INVISIBLE
YET
ENDURING
LILACS

INVISIBLE YET ENDURING LILACS

Gerald Murnane

SHEFFIELD – LONDON – NEW YORK

First UK edition published in 2020 by And Other Stories
Sheffield – London – New York
www.andotherstories.org

Copyright © 2005 Gerald Murnane
First published in 2005 by Giramondo, Australia

9 8 7 6 5 4 3 2 1

ISBN: 978-1-911508-66-3
eBook ISBN: 978-1-911508-67-0

Set in Linotype Swift Neue and Verlag by Tetragon, London.
Printed and bound in Great Britain by CPI Ltd, Croydon, on Munken Premium.

And Other Stories gratefully acknowledge that our work is supported using public funding by Arts Council England.

CONTENTS

One of the least useful tasks that a person of my years might undertake is to ask how differently he or she should have done this or that in the past.

Even so, the author of the second-last piece in this book, when he was hardly younger than I am now, chose to ask himself just that question. He answered it by declaring that he should never have tried to write novels or novellas or short stories but should have allowed each piece of his fiction to find its own way to its natural end.

The author's conjecturing is futile, of course, but it has inspired me to make an even bolder declaration. I should never have tried to write fiction or non-fiction or even anything in-between. I should have left it to discerning editors to publish all my pieces of writing as essays.

MEETINGS WITH ADAM LINDSAY GORDON

I remember an unseasonal cold in the air, an almost wintry sky, and mutterings around me from people I thought must have known the truth about the place. I knew little myself; and my father beside me was anxious, as usual, to be away.

I remember looking briefly through more than one window, but what was on the other side of the glass I do not remember. Yet I recall my childish sadness that day for things lost or detained far from their rightful surroundings. I imagined that the house itself had been shipped many years before from Britain. Hearing that a man had composed poetry behind the locked doors, I thought of the poet as a sort of prisoner there, writing to pass the months or years of his sentence or exile. And a strange chain of confusions made me think that the poet was Robert Burns, whose verses I had already chanced on – and found, of course, unreadable.

I saw Adam Lindsay Gordon's house in Ballarat only that once, on an afternoon in 1946 while I waited with my parents for the bus that would take us across the Western Plains on the second leg of our holiday journey from Bendigo to the coast. Twenty years later I looked at a photograph of the house and saw not a poet's cell or a transplanted bit of the Old World but the house where I had spent the Bendigo years of my childhood. Distracted on that grey summer day by mutterings about the poet and his unhappiness, I had not recognised the two front windows, the central front door, and the hooded iron verandah roof – the same pattern that was repeated over and over among the gravel footpaths and picket fences and pepper trees of Bendigo and every other gold-fields town.

I had failed to notice that the glass I peered through for signs of my first poet was part of the same symmetry that always appeared to me in the streets of Bendigo as a pair of eyes and a nose under a frowning forehead. Those were the eyes of all the people detained where nothing could ever be a subject for poetry or fiction. I would have seen myself as one of those blankly staring people except that my father talked often of taking us for good where we went every Christmas – south-west to his native district on the coast. Indoors on hot afternoons I never peeped around the drawn blinds of my own twin windows because I was thinking of our journey through the hills to Ballarat and then out over the plains.

I could never handle any of the *Victorian Readers*, published by the Education Department, without imagining a single personage as their compiler. It was a male, the son of a Methodist minister, with two grandparents from Birmingham, one from Aberdeen, and one from Belfast. In his youth he had worked briefly as a jackaroo. Later he had been wounded at Gallipoli. In his mature years, apart from compiling the readers, he was a bushwalker, a lay preacher, and a student of British and Imperial History and Greek and Roman mythology.

In 1949, at a two-roomed school in a forested district a little east of Warrnambool, my teacher actually looked and talked like the Compiler of Readers. And on a certain February afternoon, with his back to a window where deciduous shrubbery framed a sky hazy with bushfire smoke, he took us (his words) for poetry.

> Hark! the bells on distant cattle
>> Waft across the range,
> Through the golden-tufted wattle,
>> Music low and strange;
> Like the marriage peal of fairies
>> Comes the tinkling sound,
> Or like chimes of sweet St Mary's
>> On far English ground.

These and forty other lines from 'Ye Wearie Wayfarer' were printed in our Reader (with a new title and their stanzas altered to make them seem like a message of simple optimism). Girls who could be relied on to put feeling into their voices read aloud a stanza each. Then the composite overseer of my childhood explained that although the poet's love of beauty was apparent, still Gordon was not quite a poet to be proud of. He had not quite become an Australian. Just when the cattle-bells and the wattle should have made him appreciate the true beauty of Australia, Gordon had felt homesick for England.

I did not think it odd that Gordon should be blamed for Englishness by the same authority who taught loyalty to Empire. There were appropriate times for an Australian to think of England: during (Protestant) church services; on Shakespeare's birthday; at the funeral of a civic or military leader. In general an Australian thought English thoughts indoors and when solemnity was called for. Out of doors one could be Australian, and more light-hearted. Yet I felt a certain sympathy for Gordon. I suspected in those days that a secret meaning was hidden in the landscapes of Australia; and I thought Gordon with his simple homesickness might have been closer to that meaning than the Compiler of Readers with his breadth of outlook.

The page headed 'January' on the calendar always made me think of a yellowish plain of the Western District awash with heat haze. At the beginning of every January I foresaw myself reaching the heart of an actual plain and learning the secret that would keep me for ever afterwards contented in Australia. In January of a year when I seemed more than halfway from childhood to manhood, I found the empty paddock I had been expecting and stood there waiting to think and feel as an Australian. I was aware of nothing I could call an original thought. But if such a thought had come to me, I was sure it would have announced itself in metrical verse. I could almost hear the predictable pattern of stresses, although it had no words with it. Then, when I tried to think of myself as a poet of the Australian landscape, I had to imagine as the place where my words came to me the library of a large homestead with windows overhung by English trees. As my readers I imagined a people who strode in from the white, scorched paddocks and read leather-bound volumes in the half-light of indoors.

In a summer when I was trying not to think of poetry, because I believed I had read too much and lived too little, one of my drinking mates told me about 'Dingley Dell'. This man seemed to think of Gordon as a poet of the bush, the horseman who had once, for sheer daring, urged his mount over a fence on the edge of the steepest cliff above the lakes at Mount

Gambier. And yet this active bushman, so I was told, had shut himself away for two years at 'Dingley Dell': a lonely house on a lonely coast where convivial fellows such as ourselves would have gone mad. My drinking mate offered to take me from Melbourne to see the poet's shrine.

But we detoured too widely on the way; and somewhere near the South Australian border we were too tired and too ill to go any farther. Gordon had not been much of a drinker, but in our crazed banter we chose to confuse him with his Sick Stockrider and with a figure from Australian folk memories: the lonely, misplaced new-chum, already in the horrors from drink and maddened further by the harsh, foreign sunshine and cries of unrecognised birds.

My father, whose forebears arrived in Victoria in the 1830s, scorned all more recent migrants. But he liked to recite by heart from 'How We Beat the Favourite'. My father could forgive a good horseman much. Remembering the rhythms of racing ballads, and the internal rhymes falling like whip-blows, I looked at Gordon's poems in the first week of November this year.

Before I turned to the racing verses I looked for evidence that Gordon had looked at the Australian landscape, or felt about it, in some way peculiarly his own. I found that the poet sees his surroundings mostly as a place where he is called on to think in what he assumes to be a poet's idiom. This stanza is from the dedication to *Bush Ballads and Galloping Rhymes*.

> In the Spring, when the wattle gold trembles
>   'Twixt shadow and shine,
> When each dew-laden air draught resembles
>   A long draught of wine;

When the skyline's blue burnish'd resistance
Makes deeper the dreamiest distance,
Some song in all hearts hath existence, –
    Such songs have been mine.

Substitute an appropriate botanical term for 'wattle gold' and the poet might be in the pampas of Argentina, preparing to sing to us.

It is hardly worth raising the trite accusation that Gordon did not see Australia clearly. No doubt he saw it clearly enough for his own purposes, which did not include the writing of poems about the landscape itself. Wattles, distant mountains and horizons were boundaries of the place where poems of reflection occurred to Gordon. He was a poet in the landscape and not a poet of the landscape.

But a racecourse is a landscape – and a landscape that is no mere backdrop but an arena where many doubtful issues can be resolved. The English bookmaker and world-traveller, J. Snowy, writing not long after Gordon's death, called Melbourne the greatest horse-racing city in the world, where the entire population seemed to exist on racing. Australian writers on popular culture have made many shallow pronouncements on horse-racing. Novels and films set around racecourses seem the work of simpletons. Adam Lindsay Gordon's racing verses may be not much more than thumping doggerel, but I find it peculiarly appropriate that an early Australian poet should have put on racing silks and ridden at Flemington and Coleraine.

The racecourse must have seemed sometimes to Gordon his landscape of last resort. A man who had been born in Ballarat in the 1890s once told me that he had heard from a former jockey who rode with Gordon. At the barrier before a steeplechase one day at Dowling Forest, Gordon announced that this would be his last race. When he urged his horse like a madman at the first jump, the other riders knew what he had meant. That was the last they saw of him – in racing parlance. He won that day by a great space.

(*AGE MONTHLY REVIEW*, DECEMBER 1984)

ON THE ROAD TO BENDIGO:
KEROUAC'S AUSTRALIAN LIFE

Like other children of my time and place, I watched films from Hollywood in the first years after World War II, although I believe I watched fewer than most children. I watched perhaps twenty double-feature programmes from 1946 to 1948. The films were mostly cowboy films, in black and white, and I watched them on Saturday afternoons in the Lyric Theatre, Bendigo, of which I remember only that the floor was quite level, so that the screen always seemed high above me and remote.

The films I watched made me discontented. Scene after scene disappeared from the screen before I had properly appreciated it; the characters moved and spoke much too fast. I hardly ever got the hang of a film, as my brother would say afterwards when I asked him to explain what I had missed.

What I looked for in films was what I called pure scenery. I thought of pure scenery as the places safely behind the action: the places where nothing seemed to happen. Occasionally I glimpsed the kind of scenery I wanted. Behind the men on horses or the encampment of wagons was a broad tract of tall grass leading back to a line of hills. When I saw any such banal arrangement of grassy middle distance and hilly background, I tried to do to it something for which the simplest word I could have found was *swallow*. I wanted to feel that waving grass and that line of hills somewhere inside me. I wanted grass and hills fixed inside the space that began, as I thought, behind my eyes.

I was not so literal-minded that I was troubled by cartoon images of a greedy boy with his cheeks swollen by a segment of landscape-pie. Yet the word *swallow* was not inapt. Getting the scenery from outside to inside seemed to engage me in some kind of bodily effort. And if I did not actually think of mouth or stomach, I could still see myself crouching over scenery made somehow conveniently tiny; the scenery brought so close to my face that the familiar became blurred, and strange details filled my eyes; some crucial moment arriving for which I had no words; and finally the scenery safely mine, a piece of plain with a rim of hills floating inside my private space, and rather higher than lower, as though my space was a sort of walking Lyric Theatre and the watching part of me was on the level floor far below the screen.

But I was hardly less discontented after I had absorbed a slab of pure scenery than beforehand. Even in my private space, that scenery was still merely visible. Yet I had hoped to experience my scenery more completely. I had hoped to feel, or even to taste, the qualities that had made a plain of grass and a line of hills seem from the distance peculiarly mine. If I had been subtle enough, I might have understood that the watching part of me could do no more than watch. Even if the watching homunculus (or puerculus) had performed a further swallowing ritual, a further watcher would still have been no more than watching.

I had first been attracted to my scenery because nothing seemed to happen there; my grasses and hills were never the site of the frantic action that took place in the foreground of films. But when I was tired of waiting to understand my empty places, I allowed certain things to happen there. My scenery became the setting for most of my imagined adult life.

I spent much of my childhood assembling elaborate day-dream worlds that I thought were foreshadowings of my later life. Even at thirteen I was filling an exercise book with the pedigrees to the third generation of an imagined herd of Guernsey cattle that I intended to own one day, and with maps of my dream-farm showing how each paddock was differently stocked in each season of the year. At the same age I built from wet clay a Trappist monastery – half a span high and two metres square – and wrote down the names of all the monks, together with their roster for celebrating mass in the main chapel and the private oratories.

In my pure scenery at Bendigo I was not yet a dairy farmer or a monk. I was not even wholly I. The man of the silvery grasslands and grey-black hills was more American than Australian. His face and body were those of a cartoon-strip hero, Devil Doone. Only his thoughts were mine – or what I imagined at eight or nine would be mine twenty years from then.

That man – dark-haired, broad-chested, and quietly confi-dent – lived in a place named Idaho. As soon as I had learned to read an atlas I had discovered that in America, quite unlike Australia, a man could travel inland without confronting deserts. In a popular song broadcast from 3BO Bendigo, a chorus of sweet female voices sang of the hills of Idaho. The actual Idaho was near enough to Texas and the Santa Fe Trail to have caught the eye sometimes of a film-maker from Hollywood. And so my pure scenery led always back from the crudely imagined America of films towards the hills of my Idaho.

Far back in the seemingly empty land that was all but overlooked by the makers of American films, the Man of Idaho owned an enormous ranch. Yet the ranch, for all its size, was hardly visible from the few roads in the neighbourhood. It lay in a shallow part of the landscape, between two gentle slopes that looked from a distance like the one gradual hill. Any fool, I thought, could have located his ranch in some steep valley behind mountain peaks, like some lost world in a comic-strip adventure. But then the very mountains that were meant to hide the secret place would actually tempt and challenge intruders. The Man of Idaho laid out his ranch, his gardens, his house and the rooms inside it with cunning and pretence. Everything looked ordinary and uninviting at first glance. Bands of cowboy-actors could perform their absurd routines almost at the edge of my hero's property but quite unaware of the riches hidden from their view – just as the people around me in Bendigo could not guess what was doubly hidden inside me.

Although he was a considerable landowner, the Man of Idaho was an indoors man. I had not heard that phrase in those days; I first read it years later in an account by Hugh Hefner of *his* way of life. But the Man of Idaho was an unusual sort of playboy. The only pleasures he indulged in were the pleasures that I had decided were the most lasting and satisfying.

Two events in my childhood impressed me so deeply that I have still not traced the whole pattern of their influence in my thinking and feeling.

I was one of a line of schoolchildren shuffling through the dust under the elms in Rosalind Park and up the hill towards the Capitol Theatre to practise for our end-of-year concert. High on the hill, we climbed a wooden staircase towards the rear door of the theatre. On the last landing of the staircase, and just before I stepped into the dark theatre, I turned and looked back. Half the city of Bendigo lay below me. The shimmering iron roofs and drooping treetops, the glimpses of orange-gold gravel – everything I saw begged me to stare and interpret. I was looking at a map of the richest pleasures I knew. The long summer holidays were only days away. Anything I could fancy myself doing on blazing afternoons or in the long hot evenings – the site of it was hidden in that intricate pattern of roofs and trees.

Inside the theatre, waiting for my eyes to adjust to the dimness, I expected to feel deprived of my sight of the city. Instead, my sense of place was rearranged. I was somehow *within* the city, equidistant from every point in it, as though each place I had admired or guessed at when I saw it in the sunlight was now pressing against the outer wall of the theatre; or as though the map I had lately thought of as outspread was now shaped like one of the rings of Saturn and encircling me in the darkness. I was in the best possible position for inspecting any point I chose in the city. And for as long as I stayed in the darkness, the city would strain to press even more closely around me.

The Man of Idaho knew what I had learned in the Capitol Theatre. He knew that the way to understand a place was not to go on staring at it but to turn your back on it. The best vantage point for studying a brightly lit landscape was a dark place within the landscape. The Man of Idaho kept to his house. In the twilight behind his drawn blinds, he understood the pure scenery all around him.

Looking at Bendigo from inside out was the first of my two important events. The second was my father's putting into my hands a copy of the mid-week edition of the *Sporting*

Globe with its page of photographs of the previous Saturday's races in Melbourne.

A living racehorse stood only a few metres from where I sat looking at the *Globe*. I had helped my father feed and groom the chestnut gelding that he owned and trained; I had worn in front of a mirror the yellow and purple silk jacket and cap that comprised my father's colors; I had not yet seen a thoroughbred race run, but I had seen harness races around the showgrounds at the Bendigo Easter Fair and seen black-and-white newsreel film of abridgements of Caulfield and Melbourne cups. Until that day, though, I had not been moved by racing. Studying the pictures in the *Globe*, noting how certain horses improved their positions from the turn to the winning post while others lost ground, I began to see each race as a complex pattern unfolding. Then I thought of the spectators, each hoping for the pattern to unfold in a certain way. When I stared at a picture of a field at the turn and pretended not to have seen the same field at the finish, I could imagine many possible unfoldings of the pattern. And each race was only an item in a much larger pattern, for each horse had raced in other races in past weeks, and would add more strands to the pattern in weeks to come.

My first sight of those photographs was the beginning of my lifelong obsession with horse-racing. But what I did next was not to ask my father to take me to the next Bendigo meeting. I went into the house to devise my own sort of racing.

I began with marbles for horses and a short straight course across the floor of my bedroom to the skirting board on the far side. I steadied the marbles on the linoleum with one hand, then swept them forward with a ruler held in the other hand. The race was never satisfying. It was over too quickly; I had to shuffle across the floor beside the field, trying to observe the changing patterns and then to memorise the finishing order before placegetters and also-rans bounced back from the skirting board and milled around in a throng.

Then, on a momentous afternoon, I marked out an elliptical racecourse by scoring with a pencil the faint nap of the worn rug in the lounge room. I pushed a field of marbles forward by short stages with my eyes averted; I used my index finger to find each marble and then to nudge it forward with its fair share of force. When every marble had been sent a little way forward, I looked again at the rug. I studied the changes that had taken place in the field and wondered about each horse in turn and about the owners and trainers and supporters whose fate was bound up with the changing pattern beneath me.

The Man of Idaho was even more fond of racing than I was. As a boy he too had fingered marbles around a rug. But as a man of independent means he was free to own or train horses or even – if I could have imagined him shorter and lighter – to ride them. Instead, he shut himself away in his spacious house, in the hidden hollow of land in the pure scenery of America, and played racing games for days and weeks on end.

His racecourses were billiard-table smooth and built into the floors of his vast rooms. His horses were battery-powered toys of the quality of Hornby model trains. The jockeys wore actual silks more dainty than dolls' clothes. The forward motion of the horses during a race was imperceptibly slow, as though the Man of Idaho watched from the top level of an enormous grandstand, or as though he had more than a lifetime to appreciate his world.

In 1960 I thought I was running out of space. I wanted to be someone other than I seemed to be, and I thought I had first to surround myself with new space. Writing this today, I see that what I needed was imagined space and not, as I thought then, actual space.

I used to look at maps of Victoria, trying to find a certain country town. It was to be a town with unusually wide streets, a very large block of land for each house, a deep and shadowy verandah around each house, and behind each front door a wide passage leading back between cavernous rooms. I wanted to live in one of those rooms, with the blinds drawn. I wanted to live as a writer of fiction. My fiction would be about the people of the town, whom I would have observed from a safe distance. My books would be published under a pseudonym so that the people of the spacious town would never know I had observed them.

Sometimes I looked at maps of America, and every week I read *Time*. I had not forgotten my pure scenery or the Man of Idaho, but there was no room for dream-landscapes in the America I read about. America was for businessmen who wore buttoned-down collars or farmers who wore American Gothic costumes. Even Idaho was only a name on a map showing who was going to vote for John F. Kennedy and who for Richard Nixon.

Then I read *On the Road*. Chris Challis in *Quest for Kerouac* (1984) writes of all his friends remembering afterwards where they were and what they were doing when they first read the book that changed their lives. I can remember those details for dozens of other books that did little to me, but I have no memory of actually reading *On the Road*. The book was like a blow to the head that wipes out all memory of the recent past. For six months after I first read it I could hardly remember the person I had been beforehand.

For six months I believed I had all the space I needed. My own personal space, a fit setting for whatever I wanted to do, was all around me wherever I looked. The only catch – by no means an unpleasant catch, I thought at the time – was that other people considered my space theirs too: my space coincided at last with the place that was called the real world. But the world was much wider than most people suspected. I saw this because I saw as the author of *On the Road* saw. Other people saw the same streets of the same Melbourne that had always surrounded them. I saw the surfaces of those streets cracking open and broad avenues rising to view. Other people saw the same maps of Australia or America. I saw the coloured pages swelling like flower buds and new, blank maps unfolding like petals.

I saw all these sights in broad daylight. I pitied the boy who had tried to carry off to his private theatre the silvery backgrounds of films. I moved to the back of my writer's filing cabinet my folders of plans for imagined racecourses, my colour-pencil sketches of racing silks, my furlong-by-furlong charts of dream-races. (This, I thought in 1960, was my craziest project of all. In my sixteenth year I had suddenly gone back to my private racing-world. I needed no marbles or rug – only pen and paper. After weeks of work I had perfected a scheme in which every detail was determined by the occurrence of certain letters of the alphabet in passages of prose on pages opened at random.) Now, all I needed to do as a writer was to set down what was in front of my eyes.

I had found in *On the Road* only what I needed to find; I had learned about its author only what I needed to learn. I thought of Jack Kerouac as a man not much older than myself, doing in America in 1960 what I was doing – or about to do – in Australia. I placed him not in New York City or San Francisco but somewhere between the Mississippi and the watershed of the Rocky Mountains. I only had to think of him in Nebraska or Iowa for the grass-coloured surfaces of those places to burst out of their rectangular borders and to stretch and undulate until they covered over the old, cramped America that had seemed, from the vantage point of my childhood, to lie on the other side of Hollywood.

Six months later, so little had happened in those bloated prairie-landscapes that I had turned my back on them and looked again at what I thought I could be sure of. Later still, I began to write a novel about a city like Bendigo where a boy played with a toy racecourse that turned into the landscape of his childhood, and toy horses that turned into the competing themes of his dreams. (There was much fiction in the book. The champion racehorse was named Tamarisk Row after the trees in the boy's backyard; my own champion horse had been named Red River.) I noticed further books by Kerouac, but I thought they were all later books: books written after he had come in from the road; accounts of his ditherings in coastal cities that meant nothing to me.

I was finishing the last pages of my novel about Bendigo when I learned that Jack Kerouac had died in Florida in October 1969. I read of his death in *Time*, which had published so many harsh reviews of his books. Jack had died an alcoholic's death, and the photograph in *Time* of a bloated and dejected man seemed only a warning of what happened to those who swallowed alcohol instead of pure scenery.

A few years later the first of the biographies appeared. In 1976 I bought and read *Kerouac*, by Ann Charters. One of the appendices of this book was a chronology, the first I had seen for Jack Kerouac. Until then, I had preferred to think of Kerouac's time on the road as linked with my own years of confusion: I saw Jack as wandering vaguely westward in the late 1950s – only a few years before the hippies. (These, in their turn, were already coming in from the road in 1976 when I first read Charters.) In fact, Jack Kerouac's first trips across America had been made in the 1940s – in the years when I was watching my first American films, looking for the first time towards Idaho, arranging my first dream-racecourses.

But even before I read the chronology, I had learned what mattered much more to me. From the first chapter of Charters's book I learned that Jack Kerouac, as a boy of twelve, and about ten years before I ran my first race on the loung-eroom rug, rolled fields of marble-racehorses across the lino-leum of his bedroom in Lowell, Massachusetts. Ann Charters reported few details of the marble racing, but after I had read Dennis McNally's *Desolate Angel* (1979) and then Tom Clark's *Jack Kerouac* (1984), I understood how Jack's racing-world had been organised.

In his dream-racing, Jack had achieved much more than I had. But this statement has to be qualified. Jack was twelve years old when he ran his first races, whereas I was only seven. And I was racing marbles without having seen an actual race meeting, whereas Jack went often with his father to meetings in Boston. And the racing-world that I devised on paper at fifteen was much more elaborate than Jack's operations, although I had used it for only one meeting – recording all the details for a single race could take a whole afternoon or evening.

The chief difference between Jack's races and mine was that he had always rolled: his races were brief and hectic. Jack's marbles gathered momentum down a sloping board, then hit the floor and hurtled across the linoleum. Apparently, Jack had never thought of slow-motion races around a rug, of studying the patterns of gradual change, of prolonging his pleasure.

While his races were being run, Kerouac (baptised Jean Louis Kerouac) saw himself as Jack Lewis, owner of the racecourse, chief steward and handicapper, trainer and jockey, and owner of the greatest horse of all time, a big steel ball-bearing named Repulsion. While my marbles were arranged on the rug I was a figure rather in the background. My horse, Red River, was a dull-brown marble that had to be held up against the sunlight for its rich colour to be observed. Red River was no champion but his owner, watching the races from some tree-shaded spot at the edge of the crowd, had reason to hope that his day would come. Jack's races were run on winter afternoons to the sound of music from his wind-up record player. The only sound I heard from my place on the rug was the flapping of blinds drawn against the sun and the hot wind from inland. The racecourse was the centre of my dreams, but there were places farther off. At the end of the day, Red River and his owner went home into their pure scenery where nothing more eventful than dreaming took place.

It was nearly ten years after Kerouac's death before I read *Dr Sax*. Until I read it, I had thought I had only the biographies to tell me about the racecourse in the upstairs bedroom. Until then, in my view of America, the land was a network of the journeys and stopping places of the man who had locked away his racecourse in a gloomy room, had travelled in the same westward direction that most Americans travelled, and had seen a land like my Idaho on his travels but had passed it by.

Dr Sax was as much a shock to me as *On the Road* had been. I saw Jack Kerouac climbing up to cramped, wintry New England. I saw him look back once at the sunlit prairie states and then go into the twilight, into the place where he could see from inside out.

Everything I had wanted to know about Jack's racecourse was there, in Book Two of *Dr Sax*: detailed form guides, calls of memorable races, the sounds of glass and steel and aluminium, imagined afternoons of bright skies and a fast track, and remembered afternoons at Narragansett or Suffolk Downs among rain-sodden, thrown-away tote tickets. One more vista of America opened out for me. 'The Turf was so complicated it went on forever.'

I have mentioned only the outlines of a complicated pattern. I am still reading and re-reading Kerouac's books, and each new biography; still adding to my view of America. (I have used 'America' rather than 'USA' in this article because Kerouac was born into a French-speaking family of Canadian immigrants and because he lived for several periods in Mexico, where, in fact, he wrote *Dr Sax*.)

The latest biography, *Memory Babe* (1983), by Gerald Nicosia, is the most detailed yet. From Nicosia I learned that the adult Jack had often played a game of imaginary baseball using a pack of cards he had devised himself. He had the cards with him in 1956, during the summer that he spent as a fire-spotter, alone on Desolation Peak in Washington State.

In my own pure scenery, the far line of hills was supposed to be Idaho. But from the vantage point of the Lyric Theatre, Bendigo, Desolation Peak and the Cascades are only a few degrees to the west from Idaho. And if I have lost sight, for the time being, of the Man of Idaho, I can still see Jack Kerouac on Desolation Peak with his baseball cards, playing a game of dreams within dreams.

(*AGE MONTHLY REVIEW*, MAY 1986)

WHY I WRITE WHAT I WRITE

I write sentences. I write first one sentence, then another sentence. I write sentence after sentence.

I write a hundred or more sentences each week and a few thousand sentences a year.

After I've written each sentence I read it aloud. I listen to the sound of the sentence, and I don't begin to write the next sentence unless I'm absolutely satisfied with the sound of the sentence I'm listening to.

When I've written a paragraph I read it aloud to learn whether all the sentences that sounded well on their own still sound well together.

When I've written two or three pages I read them aloud. When I've written a whole story or a section that you might call a chapter, I read that aloud too. Every night before I start my writing I read aloud what I wrote the night before. I'm always reading aloud and listening to the sounds of sentences.

What am I listening for when I read aloud?

The answer is not simple. I might start with a phrase from the American critic Hugh Kenner . . . *the shape of meaning*. Writing about William Carlos Williams, Kenner suggested that some sentences have a shape that fits their meaning while other sentences do not.

Robert Frost once wrote: 'A sentence is a sound on which other sounds called words may be strung.'

Robert Frost also had a phrase, 'the sound of sense', to describe what he listened for in writing. Frost likened this sound to the pattern we hear when the sound of a conversation, but not the sounds of actual words, reaches us from a nearby room.

Robert Louis Stevenson had a different notion of what a sentence should do.

> Each sentence, by successive phrases, shall first come into a kind of knot, and then, after a moment of suspended meaning, solve and clear itself.

I don't say that I swear by any of these maxims that I've quoted. But each of them lights up a little part of the mystery of why some sentences sound right and some don't.

A word I haven't mentioned yet is *rhythm*. A lot of nonsense is talked about rhythm. Here's something that is far from nonsense.

> Rhythm is not an ideal form to which we fit our words. It is not a musical notation to which our words submit. Rhythm is born not with the words but with the thought. Good writing exactly reproduces what we should call the contour of our thought.

I found these words in a book published nearly sixty years ago: *English Prose Style*, by Herbert Read.

The *contour of our thought* is a magical phrase for me. It has helped me in times of trouble in the way that phrases from the Bible or from Karl Marx probably help other people.

You will not be surprised to know that Virginia Woolf had a deep insight into this matter of the rightness of sentences. Here is something she wrote about it.

> Style is a very simple matter, it is all rhythm. Once you get that, you can't use the wrong words . . . This is very profound, what rhythm is, and goes far deeper than words. A sight, an emotion, creates this wave in the mind, long before it makes words to fit it, and in writing one has to recapture this, and set this working (which has nothing apparently to do with words) and then, as it breaks and tumbles in the mind, it makes words to fit in.

Something else I listen for when I read aloud . . . I listen to make sure that the voice I'm hearing is my own voice and not someone else's voice. I don't always succeed in this, of course. Sometimes when I read my writing of a few years ago I recognise that I've imitated in a few places the voices of others.

I listen for the sound of my own voice because I remember something the Irish poet Patrick Kavanagh once said: 'This is genius – a man being simply and sincerely himself.'

And still another thing I hope to hear in my sentences is the note of authority. John Gardner said authority is the sound of a writer who knows what he's doing. He cited as his favourite example of prose ringing with authority this opening passage from a famous novel.

> Call me Ishmael. Some years ago – never mind how long precisely – having little or no money in my purse, and nothing particular to interest me on shore, I thought I would sail about a little and see the watery part of the world.

I've said I write sentences, but you probably expect me to say what the sentences are about.

My sentences arise out of images and feelings that haunt me – not always painfully; sometimes quite pleasantly. These images and feelings haunt me until I find the sentences to bring them into this world.

Note that I didn't say 'to bring them to life'. The person who reads my sentences may think that he or she is looking at something newly alive. But the images and feelings behind my words have been alive for a long time beforehand.

This has been a very simple account of something that begins to make me dizzy if I think about it for too long. The only detail I can add is to say that as I write, the images and feelings haunting me become linked in ways that surprise and amaze me. Often if I write one sentence to put into a form of words a certain image or feeling, I find as soon as I've written the sentence that a new throng of images and feelings have gathered to form a pattern where I had not known a pattern existed.

Writing never explains anything for me – it only shows me how stupendously complicated everything is.

But why do I write what I write?

Why do I write sentences? Why does anyone write sentences? What are sentences? What are subjects and predicates, verbs and nouns? What are words themselves?

I ask myself these questions often. I think about these matters every day in one way or another. For me these questions are as profound as the questions: why do we get ourselves born, why do we fall in love, why do we die?

If I pretended I could answer any of these questions, I'd be a fool.

(*MEANJIN*, VOL. 45, NO. 4, DECEMBER 1986)

SOME BOOKS ARE TO BE DROPPED INTO WELLS, OTHERS INTO FISH PONDS

The other day I stood in front of my bookshelves and stared at the spine of *Don Quixote*. According to my meticulously kept records I read that book in 1970, but when I stood staring at its spine I could remember nothing of the book itself or of the experience of reading it. I could remember no phrase, no sentence; I could not remember one moment from all the hours when I had sat with that bulky book open in front of me.

After I had waited in vain for some words from the book to come back to me, I kept a lookout for images. I waited to see some flickering scenes in black and white on the invisible screen that hangs about a metre in front of my eyes wherever I go. But not even the ghost of a scene appeared from the book. For a moment I thought I saw a silhouette of a man on horseback, but then I recognised it as a memory of the print of Daumier's painting of Don Quixote that had hung on the wall in front of where I stood until I had had extra bookshelves built there.

I gave up waiting for *Don Quixote* and performed the same test on other books. From a sample of twelve – all of them read before 1976 and never opened since – I found seven that brought nothing to mind. If this was a fair sample, then of all the books that I had read once and had not read again, more than half had been wholly forgotten within a few years. I wondered whether I was entitled to conclude that the forgotten books had been of no use to me. I wondered whether I might have better promoted my health and happiness by going for walks or doing push-ups or taking naps instead of reading those books that were going to fly away so soon from my mind. I wondered whether I might as conveniently have dropped those books down a well as read them. (Yet how could I have known at the time which books I ought to read and which books make a splash with?)

I could still not believe that so many books had left so little trace behind them. I decided that my memories of them must be buried deep. I decided to poke around in the dark places – the back rooms of my mind. I closed my eyes and said aloud over and over: '*Don Quixote*, by Miguel de Cervantes, is one of the greatest works of fiction of any age.'

While repeating these solemn words I remembered an evening in 1967 when I was a part-time student at the University of Melbourne. A lecturer in English, during a lecture on *Tom Jones*, read out in class a passage from *Don Quixote*. No doubt the lecturer was making a very important point, but I have forgotten the point today. All I remember is that the passage quoted from Cervantes was concerned with a person or persons (I think they may have been aboard a ship) being struck in the face by a quantity of wind-borne human vomit.

This seemed an odd memory to have been connected with a great work of fiction, but it was the only result of my reciting the mantra about the book. If anyone reading this has a detailed knowledge of *Don Quixote* and has never read in the great book a passage about wind-borne vomit, that person need not trouble to correct me on the point. I am not writing about *Don Quixote* but about my memory of the books on my shelves.

And now I remember one more result of my repeating aloud the words in praise of *Don Quixote*. As I said the words aloud, I became convinced that I had said them on at least one previous occasion – and not to myself, as I happened to be saying the words then, but in company. In short, I became aware that I was a person who sometimes delivered ponderous judgements on books without being able to remember any more than the name of the book, the author's name, and some judgement borrowed from someone else. This awareness made me embarrassed. I remembered people who had agreed with me when I had uttered my judgements – and people who had disagreed. I might have felt urged to seek out those people and to apologise to them. But what saved me from doing this was a suspicion that some at least of the people who had discussed the great books with me might have remembered no more about the books than I did.

Within a few days I had learned to accept myself as a man who could remember absolutely nothing about *Don Quixote* except the name of the author. I even dared to suppose the abyss in my memory might be a sort of distinction. Even the most forgetful among my friends would surely remember one passage at least from *Don Quixote*, but there I was with my memory a perfect blank. I remembered that Jorge Luis Borges had written a story with the title: 'Pierre Menard, Author of the *Quixote*'. Even Borges, with his fertile imagination, could imagine nothing stranger than that a man of our time could write the whole of *Don Quixote*; even Borges could never have supposed that a seemingly literate and civilised man could read and then *forget* the whole of the immortal work.

I became interested in the question why I remembered certain books and forgot others. I must emphasise, however, that the books I am writing about are books I have not looked into for at least fifteen years. On my shelves are many books that I read or look into every few years, and some books that I have to pick up and look into whenever I catch sight of them. My memory of these books too is strangely uneven, but for the moment I am writing about the long-forgotten and the long-remembered.

Some books that I have not read for more than thirty years have left me with images that I see nearly every day. The images are by no means comforting. I can never quite believe those people who write as adults about the joys and pleasures of their childhood reading. As a child I was made restless and unhappy by most of the books that I read. Whether the book was meant to have a happy or unhappy ending, I was always distressed by the mere fact that the book had an ending. After reading a book I would go into the back-yard and try to build a model of the landscape where the characters in the book had lived, and where they could go on living under my supervision and encouragement. Or I tried to draw maps of their houses or farms or districts, or to write in secret in the backs of old exercise books an endless continuation of the book that I had wanted not to end. Often I included myself among the characters in these prolongations.

The first book that I remember as affecting me in this way is *Man-Shy*, by Frank Dalby Davison. I first read *Man-Shy* when I was eight. I read it again soon afterwards, but I cannot remember having read it since and I could not say when I last looked between the covers of the book. What I am writing today about *Man-Shy* comes from memory; I am writing about images that have stayed with me for most of my life.

I remember the red cow. As I remember her now, the red cow stands on a hilltop in Queensland in a year not long before I was born. (My father had told me that the book was set in Queensland in the 1930s.) Probably no week of my life has passed without my seeing for a moment the red cow as she appeared in the little line drawing beneath the last lines of the text of my father's red-covered Angus and Robertson edition. I have never been to Queensland; I have never ridden a horse or seen a sheep being shorn; yet I have remembered all my life an image of a red cow on a hill in outback Queensland.

The red cow is dying of thirst. I am not going to check the text after all these years. I will quote what I have always remembered as the last words of the text. ' . . . She was about to join the shadowy herd that had gone from the ranges forever.'

Even while I typed these words just now, I felt the same painful uncertainty that I used to feel as a child. Was the red cow actual or imaginary? If the cow was actual I could at least be sure that her suffering was over. But in that case I could no longer hope that the cow I had read about would miraculously survive.

If the cow was imagined, then I wanted to ask the author what would happen to her in his imagination. Would she finally die like an actual cow? Or had the author found a way of thinking of her as alive in spite of everything?

The red cow and her calf were dying because their last waterhole had been fenced around. They were the last survivors in the wild of a herd that had been driven in from the bush to a cattle station. The owners of the station had fenced the waterholes, and the red cow and her calf were about to die from thirst.

By the age of eight I had been thoroughly taught in the eschatology of the Catholic Church. Yet nothing I had been taught could help me decide what would happen to the red cow if she died – or what *had* happened to the cow if she had already died. I knew without asking that animals lacked souls. For an animal there was no heaven or hell, only the earth. But I could not bear to think of the red cow as living on earth and then dying forever. I clung to the words on the last page . . . the red cow was going to join the shadowy herd.

I laid out in my backyard a vast savannah for that shadowy herd. I studded the savannah with waterholes. I reduced myself in size like Dollman in the comic strip. ('By a supreme effort of the will he compresses the molecules of his body and becomes . . . Dollman!') I led my shadowy herd to the waterholes and watched them drink. I stood beside the red cow while she drank unafraid from the pool at my feet.

Sometimes I left my shadowy herd in a valley while I climbed a hill to look around me. If I saw far away towards the east the cleared land and the ocean, I could still turn towards the west and see my savannah reaching far inland.

If the red cow had not been dying of thirst, she would have seen from the hill where she stood at the end of the book the edge of the blue Pacific Ocean. In that scene the blue smudge of the ocean has no other purpose than to mark the far edge of the land where the red cow has been driven to her death. For most of my life the ocean has been no more to me than a boundary marker.

Today while I think of the ocean to the east of the red cow, I am reminded of *Moby Dick*.

I have not looked between the covers of *Moby Dick* for nineteen years but I remember rather more of the book than

I remember of *Don Quixote*. This need not tell against *Don Quixote*, which I read only for pleasure whereas *Moby Dick* was one of my set texts for English at university – in the same year, as it happens, when I heard about the flying vomit in Cervantes. In 1967 I read the whole of *Moby Dick* twice through with care and some chapters more than twice.

Yet even so, *Moby Dick* has lasted well in my mind by comparison with other set texts from the same years. I can recall without effort today two sentences (one of them is the first sentence, of course), a phrase of three words, and some of the images that occurred to me while I read the text twenty years ago. I can recall also the conviction that I had while I read. I was convinced that the narrator of *Moby Dick* was the wisest and most engaging narrator I had met in fiction.

The image that comes to me from *Moby Dick* today is of a toy-like ship on a smooth, green expanse of water. The ship is not a whaling vessel but the sixteenth-century Portuguese caravel that I copied in grade seven into my history notebook from a line drawing in a textbook. On the tiny deck of the toy boat two men stand talking. A few vague figures of other men hang like monkeys in the rigging, but they are there only for decoration – none of them actually does anything. The reason for this is that all my life I have skipped over the technical terms and descriptions in all the books I have read about ships and boats; I have never understood the difference between a bosun and a capstan.

I have only just noticed that the deck of the toy ship is dotted with pots of the same shape and proportions as the pots in which cartoon cannibals cook cartoon missionaries and pith-helmeted explorers. And now, when I look again at the smooth, green water around the toy boat, I am looking not at the Pacific Ocean but at the surface of what might be a kiddies' wading pool. I can see from New Zealand to South America in one glance.

The pots are simmering on the deck because I remember having read in *Moby Dick* that the oil from the catch of the whales was boiled and purified on deck when the sea was especially calm and the weather fine. I could hardly have read that the crew kept a supply of cartoon cooking pots for this purpose, and now that I have begun this sentence I remember that the fires for heating the boiling-vessels burned in ovens made of brick. The bricks for the ovens, I have just remembered, were laid with mortar on the deck and were afterwards broken apart when they had served their purpose.

Why have I remembered just now the brick ovens on the toy ship, when for the past twenty years I thought of them as cartoon cooking pots?

In January 1987 I was halfway through writing what will be my fifth book of fiction. At the time I was not writing well. When I recognise that I am not writing well, I suppose I am staring too hard at what lies in front of my face. I try to stop staring and to notice what lies at the edges of my view. In January 1987 I had been staring for too long at soil. I was writing about a character who was staring at the soil of his native district in order to understand why he always felt drawn to that district. But then I sat back a little and noticed what was at the edge of my view. I noticed a fish pond.

The pond was not one of those bean-shaped ornamental pools overhung with ferns and pampas grass. It was a plain-looking square of bricks rising abruptly from the back lawn behind a house where I had lived for two years as a boy. As soon as I had noticed this pond at the edge of my view I knew I had found the image that would keep me writing until my book was finished. I felt as though I only had to stare at the brick walls rising out of the grass, or at the little grub-shaped bits of dried mortar still sticking between the bricks, or at the dark-green water with the raft of floating water plants whose leaves were like shamrocks – I only had to stare at these things and all the rest of the story I had been trying for three years to tell would appear to me.

It was a strange experience to discover, halfway through writing what I thought was a story about X, that I had really been writing the story of Y. I had thought for three years that I was writing a book whose central image was a patch of soil and grass, but one day in January 1987 I learned that the central image of my book was a fish pond.

It was also a strange experience just now to discover that I remembered after twenty years the brick ovens on the deck, and to see the ovens as having the shape and size of the fish pond that yielded half a book of fiction six months ago. The American poet Robert Bly once wrote that he learned to be a poet when he learned to trust his obsessions. I trusted my image of the fish pond last January and found in the image of the pond what I needed for finishing my story. I thought when I had finished the story that I had finished with the pond. I had even written into the last part of the story a description of the pond as empty of water and of the red fish that had lived in the pond as drowning in air. But now an image of the same fish pond has appeared on the deck of the *Pequod* – or, rather, many images of fish ponds have appeared on deck; and all the fish ponds are bubbling like stew pots.

Before I look into the bubbling ponds, I ask myself how I could have lived for more than thirty years without realising how full of meaning my fish pond was. I had never forgotten the pond; I would have thought of my own pond whenever I saw a pond in someone's lawn. But I had not understood how much of meaning was contained in the pond. I was given a hint sometimes, but I failed to follow it up. During most of the thirty-five years after I had left the house with the fish pond on the back lawn, I would become oddly alert whenever I noticed in a front garden a certain small variety of begonia with glossy red and green leaves. I always supposed the leaves themselves would one day remind me of something important; but I was staring at what was in front of me when I should have been watching out for things at the edge of my vision. In the house where I had lived in 1950 and 1951, a row of begonias had grown along the side fence. If I had stood and stared at those begonias I would have seen the pond from the corner of my eye.

The connection between my fish pond of 1951 and the bubbling pots on the deck of the *Pequod* is not only that the pond and the fireplaces were both of brick. The pond and the boiling oil are connected by the fact that the bricks on the deck were laid especially for the purpose and later removed.

Two years after my family had moved from the house with the fish pond, a tradesman left behind in the backyard of the house where we then lived a small heap of bricks and some unused wet mortar. While the mortar was still wet I decided I would build a small fish pond on the lawn. I wanted to have green water plants and chubby red fish in my backyard again. But after I had assembled the first row of bricks for my pond, my father ordered me to stop.

The boiling that took place in the fish ponds on the *Pequod* was for the purpose of refining the substance that the narrator of *Moby Dick* calls mostly *sperm*.

*

I wrote earlier that I remembered a sentence apart from the first sentence of *Moby Dick*. As I have remembered it for twenty years and without consulting the text, the sentence is uttered by Captain Ahab to Mr Starbuck not long before the last chase begins. An unfamiliar smell has been wafted into the noses of the two men. In my memory, Captain Ahab does a turn about the deck in the manner of Long John Silver as drawn in Classic Comics, smells the strange smell, and says, 'They are making hay in the meadows of the Andes, Mr Starbuck.'

I happen to have been born without a sense of smell. I can form no idea of the smell of hay being made. When I remember the words that I put into Captain Ahab's mouth just then, I merely see long grass growing in a place such as I have seen in photographs of the *altiplano* of Bolivia. But because I know there is something about the grassy place that I can never experience, I look at it intently, as though I might be allowed to see more in the grass than a person would see who was able to smell it.

Because I have never experienced the smelling of a thing from a distance, I suppose that a person must always be in sight of what he gets wind of. Whenever I see Ahab and Starbuck with the smell of hay in their noses I see them as in sight of land. The two men stand on the deck of their toy boat. The two are alone by now. I see no other men doing pretend-tasks or hanging idly in the rigging. The sea around the toy boat is smooth and green. I can see from end to end of the green water. The world is smaller by far than I had supposed.

Somewhere in his writings, Robert Musil reminds us of how wrong we are to think of the individual self as the one unstable item within a firm world. The opposite is the case. The unstable world drifts like an island at the heart of each of us.

When I look intently at the ocean around the *Pequod*, the green water is the fish pond. At the edge of my vision I see a grassy hill. The world is a small place by now; Queensland and South America are the one grassy hill above the pond.

The red cow smells the water. She goes down from the meadows of hay towards the pool that keeps her alive.

(*VERANDAH*, VOL. 2, 1987)

THE CURSING OF IVAN VELIKI

When I was fourteen years old I made some notes for an epic poem that I hoped to write. The poem was to have the title 'Ivan Veliki', which was also the name of its hero. The setting of the poem was to be the steppes of Central Asia. I had found the word 'Veliki' in a racebook. My hero's surname was actually the name of a mare, but the word brought to my mind an image of a young man striding through tall grass.

Ivan Veliki was the son of a lesser chieftain in one of the settled districts of the steppes. In the first canto of my poem, Ivan was to lead a small band of followers in search of a better life on the virgin lands to the east. Later cantos would describe the journey of the pioneers into the virgin lands, the founding of the new settlement, and Ivan's courting the daughter of one of his loyal advisers.

So far, the mood of the poem would have been lyrical and hopeful. But now, in the fourth and fifth canto, an ominous undertone would be heard. Unseasonal weather or idleness among some of the men or attacks of roving bands would cause hardship in the settlement. Food would become short. Young malcontents would murmur against Ivan.

My hero, having taken counsel with himself, would set out alone on a journey. When I made my notes, I had not decided on where Ivan was going. Sometimes I thought of him as searching for a Shangri-la of the steppes: a mild valley where edible mosses and lichens grew in mid-winter. Sometimes I thought he intended living as a hermit in the farthest virgin lands until his followers came begging him to return to them.

While Ivan Veliki was on his solitary journey, a delegation would arrive at the new settlement. The delegation would have been sent by Ivan's father. The old man had resented his son's leaving home and suspected that Ivan was not yet fit to be a leader of men.

The members of the delegation would be somewhat rash in their judgement. They would hear a child complaining of hunger; they would glance through the doorways of storage tents; they would listen to the glib malcontents (whose leader was Ivan's rival in love); and then they would hurry back across the steppes to Veliki Senior with a report that his son had failed as a pioneer.

When he had heard this news, the father would stride to a hillock at the edge of his settlement and would look across the miles of grass towards the virgin lands. He would raise an arm towards the sky. He would then utter part of the only line that I ever composed of all the lines and stanzas and cantos of my epic poem. The father of Ivan Veliki would shout at the sky:

'Accursed be Ivan Veliki for the shame he has brought me.'

I thought at first that these words alone would make a line of poetry, but when I recited them under my breath they seemed to lack something. And so I added a further iambic foot to the words, thereby making what seemed a satisfying metrical whole:

'Accursed be Ivan Veliki for the shame he has brought me,' he said.

I composed this line while I was walking north-west along Haughton Road towards the railway station then named East Oakleigh but now named Huntingdale. The time was early afternoon, the season was spring, and the year was 1953. For the rest of that afternoon and for a few days afterwards I thought I had achieved what was my chief ambition at that time: I thought I had become a poet.

I thought at that time and for ten years afterwards that a poet was someone who saw in his or her mind strange sights and who then found words to describe those sights. The strange sights were of value because they brought on strange feelings – first in the poet and later in the persons reading the poem. The faculty that enabled the poet to see strange sights was the imagination. Ordinary persons – non-poets – lacked imagination and saw only what their eyes showed them. Poets saw beyond ordinary things. Poets saw the virgin lands beyond the settled districts.

A few days after I had composed the first line of my epic poem, I began to tire of it and to doubt whether I was a poet after all. This process began when I looked hard at the grass to the east of the hillock where Ivan's father stood and shouted his curse. I saw that the grass of the steppes was the same grass that I had often seen on the vacant blocks of land along Haughton Road, East Oakleigh. I might have accepted this if I could have believed that the grass far away to the east of Veliki Senior – the grass of the virgin lands – was a strange sort of grass such as I had never seen with my eyes: a grass that I had imagined with my poet's imagination. But when I looked hard at the grass of the virgin lands I saw that it was the same grass that I had often seen in the paddocks of the dairy farm belonging to my father's father at The Cove, near Allansford, in south-western Victoria.

I wrote about thirty poems during the next ten years, but all of my poems irritated me when I read them. No line of my poetry brought to my mind anything but what I had already seen. At the age of twenty-three I began to write a novel. I regarded novels as inferior to poems. I thought of myself as a failed poet who had turned to prose because it was easier to write.

When I began my novel I still hoped to write about part of the strange territory that seemed to be lying all around me and just out of my view. I was more confident, now that I no longer had to worry about rhymes and metre. I wrote for three hours every night for three months. Each night before I wrote, I drank beer for two hours. While I wrote, I sipped whisky and ice-water. I hoped that the alcohol would blind me to the places that I did not want to write about and would allow my other organ of sight – my imagination – to operate.

I had hoped to write a novel about a young man growing up in a large bluestone house on a grazing property on a place resembling the pampas of Argentina. The young man would spend much of his time in the library of his house, looking out from between walls of books at the immense grasslands. In time, the young man would quarrel with his father and would leave the bluestone house and would set out for the capital city, where he hoped to become a poet.

I had hoped to write about what I thought was an imaginary house set among imaginary grasslands, but in the first scene that the beer and whisky induced me to write, a boy hardly different from my memory of myself stood on a patch of lawn behind the sandstone farmhouse belonging to my father's father. The time was the morning in 1949 when I learned that my father's father had just died. A few weeks before, my father had told me that my grandfather would soon die, after which my grandmother would probably leave the sandstone house. In that case, my father and my mother and my brothers and I would probably live in the house. The sandstone house among the paddocks of my grandfather's dairy farm had always interested me. Every day after my father had told me what he told me, I wished that my grandfather would hurry up and die.

I gave up writing my novel. During the next five years I began other novels and short stories, but a day would always come when I would seem not to be using my imagination but to be writing about what I had seen, and on that day I would give up the piece that I was writing.

I did not change overnight from ditherer to purposeful writer of fiction. During the last years before I finally wrote a novel, I stopped thinking about my imagination. I stopped thinking of myself as surrounded by a narrow zone of experience while the boundless countries of my imagination lay on its other side. I began to think of a world shaped somewhat as I would read it described twenty years later in a passage from Rilke: a world floating like an island in the ocean of the self. I began to see that I was already well qualified to write about a young man who looked for strangeness beyond what seemed ordinary.

(*BRAVE NEW WORD*, NO. 10, DECEMBER 1988)

BIRDS OF THE *PUSZTA*

The boy Clement Killeaton, the main character in *Tamarisk Row*, my first book of fiction, stares at photographs of hairy sheep and bony cattle and barefoot gipsies accompanying the article 'By Iron Steed to the Black Sea: An American Girl Cycles Across Romania' in a *National Geographic* magazine. The boy suspects that the subjects of the photograph are not real. After questioning his father, the boy understands that his suspicions are correct.

I used to look at those same photographs in the years soon after the Second World War. After I had talked to my own father about Europe, I understood what Clement understood. Europe was in every respect inferior to Australia: its farms were smaller; its farm animals yielded less; its people were less healthy and less free. I believe today that my father also believed that the people of Europe were sexually immoral and perverted, in contrast to the majority of Australians. My father sometimes reminded his sons that their forbears had left England and Ireland as early as the 1830s. Our blood was almost certainly free, my father would say, from the taints of old Europe.

As I write these sentences I am trying to think and feel what I thought and felt on days of bright sunlight in Bendigo forty years ago when I looked at grey photographs of Romania and pitied the whole continent of Europe on account of its crumbling castles and skinny animals and starving peoples, and when I suspected that my father's calling Europeans dirty meant more than that they washed irregularly. I do not believe that my thinking and feeling forty years ago was superior to my thinking and feeling today. Yet many lines in my networks of meaning lead back to the same few photographs of Romania. After forty years of reading and looking at photographs and talking to travellers, I have learned the geography of an imaginary Europe but I have somewhat neglected its history.

When I first looked at the photographs I was aware that the people and animals represented there, the houses and farms, and even the trees and grass might have been destroyed during the war. The American girl had mounted her iron steed a few years before my birth in 1939. The people I had pitied at first sight might have been dead before I saw their photographs. Whenever I thought of this possibility, I was driven to imagine the people as casting about them for a place to hide. Perhaps they had foreseen the war, or perhaps they wanted only a hiding place for indulging their strange sexual urges, but the costumed peasants and the ragged gipsies waited anxiously to hear about some secure refuge out of sight of thatched villages and walled towns.

Even if they had found some rural refuge after the iron steed had passed on its way towards the Black Sea, my Europeans might still have been killed before I had first become aware of them. In that case I was the more obliged to stare at the images that had survived them and to speculate about the last years of their lives. As a child of eight or nine years I had no way of knowing how many other people still looked at their ten-year-old copies of the *National Geographic*. There were surely days when I was the only person in Australia or any other country trying to keep alive the inhabitants of my ghost-country.

I never doubted that some of the lost Romanians had deserved their fate, and I saw in all the photographs no man or woman or child that I wanted to mourn as an individual. But I felt for the Romanians collectively what I felt for the species of birds described in my books of Australian birds as probably extinct. The men in their broad black hats and embroidered jackets and white trousers had been lost to the world as the night parrot, *Geopsittacus occidentalis*, and the noisy scrub bird, *Atrichornis clamosus*, had probably been lost. (No sighting of the noisy scrub bird had been reported since the nineteenth century. However, an amateur bird-observer exploring a gully near Albany, Western Australia, in 1961, heard a strangely loud bird-call, remembered what he had read in his bird books and discovered a small colony of the missing species. I did not read about this event until 1971, which was the year of the publication of the English translation of *People of the Puszta*, mentioned below.)

I had been interested in birds since long before I became interested in Europeans. I was no admirer of the flight of birds. I never gaped at soaring larks or gliding falcons. I was interested in the birds that I rarely saw – the birds that stayed hidden all day in scrub and foliage. Above all, I was fascinated by ground-dwelling birds – by plovers and quail and bustards. In the summer holidays in one of the years when I was still only beginning my study of Europe, I saw the nest and the eggs of a pipit, *Anthus australis*. The nest was neatly made of grass and lined with down, and the four eggs were grey-white and faintly spotted. It was the sort of nest that ought to have been hidden among thick leaves high overhead, I thought. But the pipit is a ground-dwelling bird. One of the parent-birds had flown up from the grass while I was walking with my father across a paddock in the part of Victoria known as the Western District. My father had then searched for a nest and had found it.

The finding of that nest was one of the chief events of my childhood. I no longer remember in sharp detail the nest itself or the eggs, or even the cunning placement of the nest under an overarching tussock, but I still recall my feeling when I stood looking down at the nest that something remarkable had been revealed to me.

I had read in books descriptions of the nests and eggs of every species of bird said to occupy the territory of which Bendigo was a part. I had peered up at the branches of trees every day in spring and summer in the streets of Bendigo but had seen no sign of any nest. By the time when I saw the nest in the grass I had begun to think of the nests of birds as one more of the secrets kept from the eyes of children. Sometimes, in my childish frustration, I murmured – in the sense of that word as it is used of the people of Israel in the Old Testament. Those people murmured against their God. I murmured against books. I murmured in particular against my bird books but I murmured also against books in general. I had loved books; I had believed in books; but now I murmured, and I hoped (and also feared a little) that the books would hear me.

Looking at the nest and the eggs of the pipit, I seemed to have seen something from a body of secret knowledge: I seemed to have learned something from a layer beneath the surface of the knowable. I was awed at having stumbled on something that I seemed not meant to have seen. If I had dared to touch the nest I would have seemed to myself to be offering an insult not just to the parent-birds but to something that I can only call the quality of plains.

Plains looked simple but were not so. The grass leaning in the wind was all that could be seen of plains, but under the grass were insects and spiders and frogs and snakes – and ground-dwelling birds. I thought of plains whenever I wanted to think of something unremarkable at first sight but concealing much of meaning. And yet plains deserved, perhaps, not to be inspected closely. A pipit, crouched over its eggs in the shadow of a tussock, was the colour of dull grass. I was a boy who delighted in finding what was meant to remain hidden, but I was also a boy who liked to think of lost kingdoms.

On the day when we found the nest, my father and I were on the outward leg of a short journey. Knowing we would come back that day by the same route, we spiked the tallest stem of a clump of rushes through a sheet of paper to mark the site of the nest. Later that day we returned to the place where our marker fluttered. I had said I wanted to inspect the nest and the eggs once more, but when I strode to where I thought the nest lay, I could not find it. My father and I walked backwards and forwards over the area around the marker. At each step I stared down at the grass and took pride in my learning the secrets of plains. At each step I gloated over the nest that I could not find and would never see again.

Since my return in 1951 to Melbourne, where I was born, I have mostly thought of myself as being surrounded by grasslands. I think of an inner arc of actual grasslands such as the plains from Lara through Sunbury to Whittlesea. Then I think of a further and more sweeping arc of grasslands in a vague area on the far side of the Great Dividing Range. This arc, provided that I have no maps nearby to confine my thinking, reaches from Camperdown through Maryborough and then around through Rochester towards Shepparton.

Beyond these two concentric arcs of grass is foreign territory. Whenever I think of myself as being forced, for whatever reason, to flee from my native district, I think of myself as fleeing into the grasslands. In desperate circumstances I might flee as far as the outer grasslands, but I could never see myself as fleeing further.

I think of myself as having learned from ground-dwelling birds how to preserve myself: how to go to earth on grasslands. I have never been so anxious that I have not been able to think of myself as being saved by my grasslands.

And yet I have suspected for most of my life that grasslands may not be a secure refuge. In the first days of my reading my bird books, I thought often about the species described as extinct or probably extinct. Of these species I thought most often about the bustard, *Eupodotis australis*, which had once been common on the plains around Melbourne but was no longer found there.

I thought of the Romanians in my photographs as a rare species. I wondered what grasslands they might have fled to. The photographs showed more mountains than grasslands, but I thought of the mountains of Europe as I thought of the mountains to the east and the north-east of my native district. The mountains were too obvious a place to hide in.

One photograph in my *National Geographic* showed two hundred men and women arranged in concentric circles for an elaborate, slow-moving dance called the *hora*. The men and women were arranged in circles on grass. The photo-graph showed as background nothing but grass – a field of grass under a wide sky. The photograph had been taken as though to suggest a great sweep of grass, but I could not accept that a true grassland could be found in Europe. The dark faces under the hats and scarves seemed troubled by a European sadness. The people in the photograph could see what I could only surmise. From where they shuffled on the grass the Romanians could see, just out of the zone of the photograph, some decrepit village where children with scabs on their faces hung out of dark doorways, or some roadside camp of gipsies with stringy hair. The slow, sad dancers longed for a true grassland.

The dancers shuffled across the grass. When the American girl had taken her photograph from beside her iron steed, the grass had already been trampled. I saw no tussocks where a bird might have sheltered. If the ground-dwelling birds of Australia had almost all gone from their grasslands, where were the birds of the trampled grasslands of Europe?

In 1971 I bought for my children an encyclopedia of the animal world. Under the heading *Bustard* I read about the Great Bustard of Eurasia. I read that the species had become extinct in Britain in the 1830s and was no longer seen in populated areas of the Continent. In 1971, if I looked towards Europe from my vantage point on the edge of the grasslands north of Melbourne I saw only populous river valleys or uninviting mountains.

What I read about the Great Bustard was written in the present tense. I read about the elaborate courtship dances that the male bustard performs in front of the female in a broad clearing among the grass. But I saw the male as a ghostly outline drifting around an almost-invisible female. I saw the birds in the same way that I see ghostly American men and women when I read texts in the present tense written by anthropologists – ghostly Americans such as the men and women who fish and hunt and farm on islands in the mouth of the Hudson River.

In another article in the encyclopedia, under the heading *Courtship Display*, I read that experimenters had observed male bustards performing their elaborate dance in front of effigies each made by attaching the severed head of a female to a short pole. I included this fact in a paragraph in my third book of fiction, *The Plains*. Some years after that book had been published, I received a letter from the director of a small dance company asking my permission to read aloud short passages from my book during a performance of several dances. One of the passages was the paragraph reporting the dance of the male bustard in front of the effigy of the female.

I believe nowadays that I considered the people of Europe less than real during my childhood because they had no grasslands where they could have discovered the nests of ground-dwelling birds and where the people themselves could have dreamed of hiding themselves if they had to flee.

In the summer of 1986–87, while I was writing my fifth book of fiction, *Inland*, I asked myself what I remembered most clearly from all the books of fiction that I had read. I decided that I remembered most clearly and with most pleasure what I call spaces-within-spaces.

I decided that what I remembered most clearly from the work of fiction that I admire most, *Remembrance of Things Past*, is my understanding the Narrator as the man with two Ways running through him – the Guermantes and the

Méséglise. I remember the Narrator as a man made up mostly of landscapes and urged to study those landscapes until the impossible takes place in front of his eyes and the many landscapes and the two Ways merge to form the whole of a private country – his true homeland.

I decided that I remembered most clearly from the book that I admire most among books of fiction in the English language, *Wuthering Heights*, a scene near the end of the book. Mr Lockwood, now living far from the North, is invited by a friend back to that district to shoot grouse on the moors. At a roadside inn in the North, Lockwood observes an ostler looking at a cart of green oats passing by. The ostler speaks:

> Yon's fraugh Gimmerton, nah! They're allas three wick' after other folk wi' ther harvest.

This scene has haunted me since I first read *Wuthering Heights* as a schoolboy thirty years ago. I am fascinated by the *shape* of what takes place. A man visits a remote district. In that district the man sees a sign of a further district that seems as remote and harsh to the people around him as their district seems to him. Then the man remembers that the further district is linked with his own past.

> 'Gimmerton?' I repeated – my residence in that locality had already grown dim and dreamy.

In the further district, so the man remembers, is a house where he once lived, a woman he once thought of falling in love with, a tribe of people with their own joys and sorrows, and a bleak and distinctive landscape.

Writing this today, I was struck for the first time by the fact that Mr Lockwood is returning to the moors for the purpose of destroying ground-dwelling birds. This sent me to a passage in Chapter 12 in which Catherine Linton, née Earnshaw, lies in bed at Thrushcross Grange handling feathers from her pillow and remembering the birds of the moors. She remembers especially the ground-dwelling lapwing and a clutch of young lapwings that had died because Heathcliff had set a trap over their nest.

From this passage I turned to two passages in *Inland* describing the killing of birds. For most of the time while I was writing *Inland* I was thinking of the characters in *Wuthering Heights*. Only today I understood that I must have had in mind also the birds of that book.

The spaces-within-spaces are not only landscapes within landscapes. When I remember *The Trial* and *The Castle* or even *The Man Without Qualities*, I am looking in each case across a huge room towards a doorway into another huge room. Without being able to see into the further room I understand that further doorways open from that room into other huge rooms. Chairs and coffee tables and grand pianos and marble busts are arranged around the walls of the room where I stand, but the vast space of floor at the centre of the room is bare. I hear from somewhere among the further rooms a crowd of people talking and laughing. The noise grows louder. I think of the roar of an incoming sea. I can see no place to hide myself in the huge room, but I set out hopefully through a doorway at the side. I am hoping to find the one room among the hundreds of rooms where I can hide safely. I am hoping to reach the library.

*

The first picture that I saw of a Hungarian was not of an actual person but of a stuffed effigy – an outsize man of white cloth strung high between two trees that looked like poplars. This picture also had been taken by the American girl. I had been annoyed in the 1940s to learn that the boundaries of Europe were untidy: that thousands of Hungarians lived in Transylvania.

The effigy was of a bridegroom. In the white-walled farm-house below the poplar-like trees, a wedding was being celebrated. As I recall it, the photograph showed no one connected with the wedding. All I remember are the white farm buildings under a grey sky, the tall trees, and the white monster-mummy hanging.

Today, as I wrote the paragraph above, I realised for the first time that most of the details I saw forty years ago in the first photograph I saw of things Hungarian – most of those details are important items in *Inland*, part of which is set in a country like Hungary. The white farm buildings, the poplar-shaped trees, the American girl behind the camera – these I recognised at once as belonging in *Inland*. I did not see at once that the blank-faced figure hanging in the trees, the dummy-bridegroom, is the narrator of my book.

I learned while I was still a child about the Hungarian grassland, the *puszta*. The first picture that I saw of the *puszta* I have forgotten, perhaps because the caption included the words *Hungarian cowboys* to describe a group of horsemen. The word cowboy would have made me consider the men of the *puszta* imitation *Americans* and therefore doubly inferior to Australians by my father's and my own standards of horsemanship.

In time, however, the few pictures that I saw and the references that I read to the terrain of Hungary led me to think of Hungarians rather than Romanians when I wanted to think about Europe. The Hungarians had a grassland, even though I thought of the grass on the *puszta* as short and trampled like the grass where the Romanians had danced the *hora*, and even though I never thought of any ground-dwelling birds nesting on the *puszta*. When I had learned that the Magyars had migrated to the *puszta* from somewhere in Central Asia, the people of Hungary seemed to me at last a real people: the first people I had been able to imagine as real from among the peoples of Europe. The trampled *puszta*, the actual grassland of Hungary, was not for the Hungarians their grassland of last recourse. When the Hungarians stared at the *puszta* they might have been dreaming of another grassland far away – a grassland of grasslands.

In 1976 I read *People of the Puszta*, a book of non-fiction by Gyula Illyés. I learned from the first page of that book that in Transdanubia, where Illyés was born, the word *puszta* refers to the collection of buildings belonging to the farm servants on a great country estate. I had opened the book expecting to read about the people of the grasslands, but I was reading about oppressed farm servants in the low hills west of the Danube before the Great War. Yet I owe to my reading of *People of the Puszta* my writing of *Inland*.

Two details from *People of the Puszta* stayed with me afterwards until I was driven to turn them into a book of fiction. The two were an account of the drowning of a young woman in a well and the author's penetrating as a man the libraries and drawing rooms of the same manor houses that had seemed awesome fastnesses when he had been the son of oppressed farm labourers.

*

After I had read *People of the Puszta*, but before I had begun to write *Inland*, I read *A Time of Gifts* by Patrick Leigh Fermor. I began the book knowing that the author as a young man in 1933 had set out to walk from the Netherlands to Istanbul. I believed *A Time of Gifts* would describe all the stages of that journey, but then I noted that the last chapter was called 'The Marches of Hungary'. I was to be conducted to the border of Hungary and no further. And so I was. *A Time of Gifts* ends with the author on the bridge over the Danube at Esztergom.

At the end of the text were the words TO BE CONTINUED. I began to inquire after the sequel. This was several years after *A Time of Gifts* had been first published, but I was told that no sequel had appeared.

In 1985 I was still looking out for the book that would take me into Hungary, but I did not even know whether Patrick Leigh Fermor, who had been born in 1915, was alive or dead. By then I had begun my own book about the grasslands of Europe. At some time in 1986, while I was finishing *Inland*, *Between the Woods and the Water* was published in England. I was aware of this event, but by then I would not have dared to read Fermor on Hungary. I wanted *Inland* to be my own book of my own images of my own country.

The narrator of the first part of *Inland* is a man in a library of a manor house on a grassland rather like the *puszta*. If I had read Fermor while I was writing that section of *Inland* I might have been led into thinking that the narrator of my book ought to resemble some man who had actually lived in Hungary, whereas I wanted my narrator to be the sort of man who could only appear in a book written by a man who knew very little about the country that Patrick Leigh Fermor had walked across.

Yet sometimes, while I wrote, I could not help thinking about the country that I was going to read about when *Inland* was finished and when I opened my copy of *Between the Woods and the Water*. At one such time I was thinking of writing that the man in the library of the manor house was thinking of bustards. I was thinking that the man might have remembered having seen bustards as a child on the grasslands near his estates. Perhaps the father of the man had found the nest of a bustard while the two of them were out riding one day. Or the man in the library might have remembered having tried to tame bustards on the lawns around his manor house many years before. But I wrote about no bustards in *Inland*. I remembered that I had once supposed that the Great Bustard no longer inhabited the grasslands of Europe. And I remembered that I had written about bustards in my third book of fiction, *The Plains*. In that book a young woman feeds a flock of half-tame bustards while a man watches her from the windows of a library.

This piece of writing began as a review of *Between the Woods and the Water*, but it has turned into something else. Perhaps it will seem more like a review if I end by quoting a long passage from Fermor's book. I could have quoted from almost any page of the book in order to show that Patrick Leigh Fermor is a superb writer. But I am quoting from a certain passage in order to show that some books are magical.

> I half-wished, when I set off, that my plans were leading me in another direction . . . But I had been swayed by the old maps in the library the day before and there were satisfactory hints of remoteness and desolation in the south-eastern route I was actually taking. A hundred years ago this stretch

of the Alfold resembled a vast bog relieved by a few oases of higher ground. Hamlets were grudgingly scattered and . . . many of these were nineteenth-century settlements which had sprung up when the marsh was drained. The air of desolation was confirmed by those tall and catapult-like sweep-wells rearing their timbers into the emptiness . . .

I found him strolling in the avenue that led to the house. He must have been about thirty-five. He had a frail look, a slight tremor, and an expression of anguish – not only with me, I was relieved to see – which a rather sorrowful smile lit up. A natural tendency to speak slowly had been accentuated by a bad motor-crash brought about by falling asleep at the wheel. There was something touching and very nice about him, and as I write, I am looking at a couple of sketches in the back of my notebook; not good ones, but a bit of this quality emerges.

German was his only alternative to Magyar. He said, 'Come and see my Trappen!' I didn't understand the last word, but we strolled to the other side of the house where two enormous birds were standing under the trees. A first glance suggested a mixture of goose and turkey but they were bigger and nobler and heftier than either and, at a closer look, totally different; the larger bird was well over a yard from beak to tail. His neck was pale grey with a maroon collar, his back and his wings a speckled reddish buff and strange weeping whiskers swept backwards from his beak like a slipstream of pale yellow Dundrearies. Their gait was stately; when our advent sent them scuttling, Lajos made me hang back. He approached them and scattered grain and the larger bird allowed his head to be scratched. To Lajos's distress, their wings had been clipped by the farmer who had found them the month before, but when the larger bird opened his, and then spread a fine fan-shaped tail like a turkey's he looked, for a moment, completely white, but then turned dark again as he closed them. They were Great Bustards, rare and wild birds that people wrongly relate to the Ostrich. They love desolate places like the puszta and Lajos planned to keep them till their feathers had grown enough for them to fly away again. He loved birds and had a way with them, for these two followed him up the steps with a stately pace, then through the drawing-room and the hall to the front door and, when he shut it, we could hear them tapping on it from time to time with their beaks.

Some books are not to be murmured against.

(*SCRIPSI*, VOL. 5, NO. 1, 1988)

PURE ICE

One hot afternoon in the summer of 1910, or it may have been 1911 or even as late as 1917 or 1918 . . . one hot afternoon in one of those years when my father was still a schoolboy at Camperdown in the Western District of Victoria or at Crabbes Creek in the Murwillumbah district of New South Wales or at Allansford on the Hopkins River and back again in the Western District of Victoria (you will notice that my father, like the father of one of the characters in *Inland*, led a wandering life) . . . one hot afternoon in the summer of one of those years more than seventy years ago, it was a freezing night on the other side of the world.

It was a freezing night on the other side of the world because, as every schoolboy knows (and even the wandering schoolboy who later became my wandering, eccentric father would have known in 1910 or 1918 or whenever it was) . . . as every schoolboy knows, things happen the wrong way round on the other side of the world.

On the other side of the world (where my father, for all his wandering, never dreamed of going and where I have sometimes dreamed of going but will never go) . . . on the other side of the world, things happen such as a decent Australian schoolboy (which I believe my father to have been and which I believe he believed me to be) . . . things happen such as a decent Australian schoolboy can hardly imagine. For example, on cold nights in winter on the other side of the world, snow falls out of the sky and ice forms on the water in wells.

My father travelled in every state of Australia during his fifty-five years but he kept to the plains and the river basins, and so he never saw snow falling. I have travelled much less widely than my father and yet I *have* seen snow falling. I saw snow falling faintly on my schoolground for a few minutes on a winter day in 1951.

Among you people here today, the few people who have already read *Inland* will understand the importance of what I am about to say. Those people will know that one of the many themes of the book is the theme of Australia's having been corrupted by Europe. My father believed all his life that Australia had been corrupted by Europe. My father tried all his life to avoid the evils of Europe. He believed that snow was one of the evils of Europe. I had no reason for disagreeing with him.

Before I began to write this text I knew that I had seen snow falling somewhere once in my life. Not until a few minutes ago did I pause to consider where I had seen the European stuff falling out of the sky.

I saw snow falling on the suburb of Pascoe Vale, which is about ten kilometres north from the city of Melbourne and about three kilometres west of the place where I was born. The snow fell lightly on a winter day in 1951. The snow fell for only a few minutes, but afterwards I found small heaps of frozen stuff in corners of the schoolground. I was so unused to snow that I called the frozen stuff *ice*. I had thought it was snow while it was falling, but when I found it on the ground I called it ice.

I wish I had remembered while I was writing *Inland* what I only just remembered while I was writing this text. The people here today who have read *Inland* can imagine what meaning I could have found in the fact of snow – pure, white, corrupt, European snow – having fallen on Pascoe Vale, on the suburb where the red fish lived in the green pond, in the year 1951 of all years.

One hot afternoon in Australia more than twenty years before I was born, it was, as I said before, a freezing night in Europe. It was not a night to be out in. And any person who had to be out on that night ought not to have been barefoot.

I often think of that night on the other side of the world. I often try to see in my mind a district of low hills south-west of the Great Plain of Hungary. It is hard to see in your mind a place where you have never been, as it was on a night more than twenty years before you were born. Sometimes I read the words of a man who heard on many a night in his childhood some of the sounds that might have sounded on the night that I often think about.

> Rarely did I succeed in catching something of the mystery. Somewhere a mother called her daughter. 'Kati-i!' . . . and in the long, drawn-out cry something of the mystic charm drifted along under the vertiginously high stars. There was no answering cry. One of the pigs grunted once or twice and the hens flapped their wings in the coops.

The passage quoted is from *People of the Puszta*, by Gyula Illyés, translated by G.F. Cushing and published in 1971 by Chatto and Windus. *People of the Puszta* is not a book of fiction.

It was a hard night to be out in, but a young woman – scarcely more than a child – was out on that night, and she was barefoot. She ought not to have been barefoot. She was the owner of a pair of boots. But she had left her boots behind her in her hurry to be out on that night.

While the young woman was out on that night, certain sounds sounded such as did not usually sound on cold nights in that part of the world. The sounds were not heard by the boy who grew into the man who wrote the book called in English *People of the Puszta*. But on his way to school next morning the boy saw on the icy ground a sight that would have enabled him to hear in his mind on that morning, and many times during the rest of his life, the sounds that had sounded on the cold night. The sight that the boy saw on the icy ground is described in his own words translated from the Magyar language into the English language on page 188 of *People of the Puszta* and on page 161 of *Inland*.

The boy who saw the sight on the icy ground on his way to school grew up to become a writer of books. His books were all in the Magyar language, but one of the books was translated into the English language, and I happened to read that book in 1976.

After I had read the book I tried often to see in my mind the sight that the boy had seen on the icy ground on that morning more than twenty years before I was born. I also tried to hear in my mind the sounds that might have sounded on the cold night before the cold morning. At some time I began to believe that some of those sounds might have been words. I knew that the words would have been words in the Magyar language, but I began to believe that I understood what the words would have been in the English language. As soon as I began to believe this, I began to write *Inland*.

Of the three people that I named a little while ago as being alive on the freezing night, which was a summer afternoon in this part of the world . . . of the three people, the schoolboy who became my father, the schoolboy who became the writer of books in the Magyar language, and the young woman, hardly more than a girl, who had left her boots behind . . . of those three people all are now dead. But while I was reading *Inland* I began to think of those people as alive. Today, more than a year after my finishing the writing of *Inland*, I continue to think of those people as alive.

I have sometimes been able to suppose that my father has read, translated into the language of ghosts, certain pages the writing of which pages caused me to think of my father as alive.

I have sometimes been able to suppose also that the writer of books in the Magyar language has read, translated into the language of ghosts, certain pages the writing of which pages caused me to think of the writer of books in the Magyar language as alive.

I have never been able to suppose that the young woman who left her boots behind in her hurry to be out in the freezing night . . . I have never been able to suppose that that person has been able to read – even in the language of ghosts – any pages of mine.

Many times during the three years while I was trying to write the book now called *Inland*, I had almost decided that I could not finish the book. At those times I used to urge myself to go on writing by seeing in my mind myself sitting in front of a group of people such as you people here today. I used to see myself sitting as I am sitting here, and I used to hear myself saying in the English language, but as though my words would be heard in the language of ghosts by a person who would never read my pages – not even in the language of ghosts – because she had never been taught to read words written or printed on pages . . . I used to hear myself saying, at last, 'Your book has been published; your story has been told.'

(TEXT OF A SPEECH GIVEN BY GERALD MURNANE AT THE LAUNCHING OF *INLAND* IN ADELAIDE ON 9 MARCH 1988; PUBLISHED IN *MERIDIAN*, VOL. 7, NO. 2, OCTOBER 1988)

THE TYPESCRIPT STOPS HERE:
OR, WHO DOES THE CONSULTANT CONSULT?

The statement in the title may be misleading. No typescript stays for long on my desk. As soon as I've written a page or so of comments I send typescript, comments and my recommendation back to the editor. Yet my desk is the end of one road for many a promising piece of fiction. The author, perhaps the friends or advisers of the author, perhaps a literary agent – these people have considered the typescript worth sending to *Meanjin*. The editor and assistant editor of *Meanjin* have read the typescript and have liked it. Then the typescript has been passed on to me, and soon afterwards – sometimes as soon as I've read the first couple of pages – the way to publication in *Meanjin* has been blocked off.

Meanjin has a poetry editor but a fiction consultant. The difference may not be clear to every reader. The poetry editor receives all the poetry submitted to *Meanjin* and is wholly responsible for deciding which poems are published. As fiction consultant I receive only a selection of the fiction submitted to the editor.

About 700 pieces of fiction were submitted to *Meanjin* during 1988. Each of these pieces was read by the editor; many were read by the assistant editor also. About a hundred pieces of fiction were passed on from the editor to me. Of these hundred I recommended about twenty-five for publication. Among the remainder I found about a dozen promising enough for me to suggest to each author that the piece might be publishable after it had been rewritten.

I sometimes remind myself that about 600 typescripts of fiction were returned to their authors during 1988 without my having learnt even the titles of the pieces or the names of the authors. Perhaps a few of the 600 stories that I did not see during 1988 might have impressed me more than they impressed the editor or her assistant, but I have never wanted to change the system. I could not find the time to read, let alone to comment on, any more typescripts than I receive already. Besides, I like the checks and balances of the present system. When I take a liking to a story by an unpublished writer, I know that at least one competent judge has already liked the story.

The question in the title would seem to have been answered by now: as consultant, I consult no one. Yet the matter is not so simple. At the moment when I look for the first time at a piece of short fiction, I find myself performing what might almost be called a mental exercise: I find myself consulting my better self.

In 1980 I became a full-time lecturer in fiction-writing at a college of advanced education. In each year since then I have had to assess between 300 and 400 pieces of students' fiction, each piece being of about 2,000 words. I mention this not by way of boasting or complaining but because it has to be mentioned. I have to mention also that I not only read each story from each student; I edit each story and write detailed comments on it. After I've spent an hour on a story I sometimes cut short my comments but not my editing. The average story takes about an hour and a half to assess in this way.

People who hear from me what I've just written often ask me whether my tasks as a teacher of fiction bore me. I answer that I'm often bored while I'm reading a student's story. I say that I'm often irritated and sometimes exasperated. But then I say what is the point of these paragraphs about my teaching duties. I say that I always feel a certain pleasure when I pick up a student's story for the first time; I feel expectant and hopeful. After I've read the first few paragraphs I may be already bored or even irritated, but while I'm preparing to read a story for the first time I'm hopeful that my pleasure will continue.

As a teacher of fiction-writing I assess each piece of fiction by registering the persistence, or the decline, or the decline followed by the resurgence, of the pleasure that I felt when I began to read the first sentence. As fiction consultant for *Meanjin* I do somewhat the same. The comments that I type while I read each story for *Meanjin* are similar to the comments that I write in the margins and on the verso pages of each student's story. Occasionally a student complains that my comments have a harsh tone. I answer that I was trying to express through my comments not harshness but disappointment. Occasionally an author complains to the editor of *Meanjin* about my comments. I have not time for entering into correspondence with any author, but I hereby state that I pick up each typescript hoping that I'll be surprised and delighted and hoping that I'll have to write only the one comment: 'Recommended for publication.'

When I prepare to read a piece of fiction I look forward to learning something that the author could have told me by no other means than the writing of the piece of fiction in front of me.

When I prepare to read a piece of fiction I look forward to reading something that is true in a way that no piece of scientific writing or philosophical writing or biographical writing or even autobiographical writing can be true. The narrator of 'Landscape With Freckled Women' in my book of fiction *Landscape With Landscape* speaks for me when he claims that he can never be sure of the truth of any words except the words spoken by a character in a work of fiction whose narrator has declared that the character in question is speaking truthfully.

When I speak or write about what I call *true fiction*, some people suppose that I think of the best fiction as a sort of confessional writing. I deny this. What I call true fiction is fiction written by men and women not to tell the stories of their lives but to describe the images in their minds (some of which may happen to be images of men and women who want to tell the truth about their lives).

My experience has been that a writer begins to write a piece of true fiction not knowing what he or she is trying to explain. In the beginning, the writer knows only that a certain image or cluster of images seems to mean something of importance. At some time after the writing has begun, the writer begins to learn what that meaning is. The writer goes on learning while he or she writes. Sometimes the writer is still learning after the writing has been finished or even after it has been published. My experience has been that a writer has to trust his or her better self in order to write true fiction.

Readers of ill will may suppose that I use the term *better self* for something that they call the unconscious. Readers of ill will seldom understand any statement not in accordance with fashionable theories of psychology or politics or economics. Readers of good will will understand me when I write that my better self is the part of me that writes fiction in order to learn the meaning of the images in my mind. The same readers will understand me when I write that my better self is the part of me that reads fiction in order to learn the meaning of the images in other minds.

Most stories passed on to me from the editor of *Meanjin* have covering notes or letters attached. I try to separate the text of the fiction from its attachments without learning even the name of the author. I prefer to be influenced only by the sentences of the text.

I read slowly the first sentence of each story. I hear in my mind the sounds of the words and I feel in my mind the rhythms of the sentence as a whole. While I read the first sentence, images appear in my mind. Most of the images have to do with the words of the sentence, but one image seems to lie on the far side of the other images. The far image is at first more a ghostly outline than a clear image. The far image is the outline in my mind of the person who is the source of the sentence in front of my eyes.

If the first sentence of the text has been a clear and honest sentence, if the sentence has persuaded me that the writer wrote the sentence in order to describe simply and honestly an image or a cluster of images in his or her mind with the aim of learning in due course the meaning of the image or images, then I begin to believe that the image of the person forming behind the other images in my mind will be an image of the better self of the person. In that case also, I begin to feel towards the better self whose image has begun to form in my mind an attitude of trust.

The term *better self* in the context of this article is a term that I devised myself. I had thought of using the term 'implied author', which is used by Wayne C. Booth in his book about techniques of narration, *The Rhetoric of Fiction*, but whereas all better selves of writers are implied authors, not all implied authors seem to me the better selves of the writers. I use the term *better self* for any implied author that I feel inclined to trust on the grounds that he or she seems to have written from the best of motives. The previous paragraph should have made clear what I regard as the best of motives for writing fiction.

If the first sentence of the text has been a clear and honest sentence, then I begin to read the second sentence. If the first sentence has not been clear and honest, then the images in my mind will be blurred and the implied author of the sentence will not yet have earned my trust. In that case, instead of beginning to read the second sentence I begin to write the first sentence of the page or so of comments that I address to the editor of *Meanjin* for the benefit of the author. I may write that the first sentence has seemed vague or unclear or stilted or pretentious. If I write such a comment, I try to explain which word or phrase or which fault in the shape of the sentence caused me to write the comment.

I go on reading sentence after sentence and writing a comment whenever a sentence has disappointed me. Sometimes, after having read only the first couple of pages, I decide that the story is not interesting enough to be published in *Meanjin*. To put the matter more bluntly, I decide that the story is too boring to be published in *Meanjin*.

Some readers of this article may be surprised to read that the fiction consultant for a publication with the prestige of *Meanjin* uses for his criteria such everyday terms as *interesting* and *boring*. Perhaps those readers will be less surprised if I add that I'm interested, as a reader, in whatever the writer is truly interested in and that I'm bored, as a reader, by anything that bores the writer. Many of the disappointing stories that I read during 1988 seemed to have been written by authors who chose their subjects only because they seemed subjects that would impress an editor or a fiction consultant.

An interesting story convinces me from the first few sentences that the author has written the story in order to discover the meaning of some part of his or her experience. (If any person concludes from this that I prefer to read stories written in the first person or stories that are obviously autobiographical, then that person has not begun to understand what I am saying here.) A boring story usually puts me in mind of an author who is confused or vain or anxious to impress or who thinks that *Meanjin* stories have to be about the things that some journalists call *issues* or have to have characters who talk about ideas.

The most common fault that I found during 1988 in stories by previously published writers was shoddy sentences – sentences that seemed to have been dashed down and never read aloud, let alone revised, sentences seemingly unconnected with human thoughts or feelings. Stories by previously unpublished writers most commonly made me suspect that the writers were nervous – that they had not yet learnt the value of their own memories and dreams and thoughts and feelings as material for fiction.

The two best means that I've found for helping students of fiction-writing are to comment on their stories sentence by sentence and to discuss with them some of the practical accounts that writers of fiction have written about their craft. Of the many of these, I quote to students most often a single sentence by Isaac Bashevis Singer. Often during 1988 when

I was trying to explain to an author that his or her story was not interesting enough for *Meanjin*, but trying at the same time to encourage the author to write a better story, I found myself quoting the same sentence to the rejected author.

The sentence goes: 'Before I write a story, I must have a conviction that it is a story that only I can write.'

(*MEANJIN*, VOL. 48, NO. 1, 1989)

I first read part of the novel *À la recherche du temps perdu*, translated into English by C.K. Scott Moncrieff, in January 1961, when I was aged a few weeks less than twenty-two years. What I read at that time was a single paperback volume with the title *Swann's Way*. I suspect today that I did not know in 1961 that the volume I was reading was part of a much larger book.

As I write these words in June 1989, I cannot cite the publication details of the paperback volume of *Swann's Way*. I have not seen the volume for at least six years, although it lies only a few metres above my head, in the space between the ceiling and the tiled roof of my house, where I store in black plastic bags the unwanted books of the household.

I first read the whole of *À la recherche du temps perdu*, in the Scott Moncrieff translation, during the months from February to May in 1973, when I was thirty-four years old. What I read at that time was the twelve-volume hardcover edition published by Chatto and Windus in 1969. As I write these words, the twelve volumes of that edition rest on one of the bookshelves of my house.

I read a second time the same twelve-volume edition during the months from October to December 1982, when I was forty-three years old. Since December 1982, I have not read any volume by Marcel Proust.

Although I cannot remember the publication details of the volume of *Swann's Way* that I read in 1961, I seem to remember from the colours of the cover a peculiar brown with a hint of underlying gold.

Somewhere in the novel, the narrator writes that a book is a jar of precious essences recalling the hour when we first handled its cover. I had better explain that a jar of essences, precious or otherwise, would be of small interest to me. I happen to have been born without a sense of smell. That sense which is said by many persons to be the most strongly linked to memory is a sense that I have never been able to use. However, I do have a rudimentary sense of taste, and when I see in my mind today the cover of the paperback of *Swann's Way* that I read in 1961, I taste in my mind tinned sardines, the product of Portugal.

In January 1961, I lived alone in a rented room in Wheatland Road, Malvern. The room had a gas ring and a sink but no refrigerator. Whenever I shopped, I looked for foods that were sold in tins, needed no preparation, and could be stored at room temperature. When I began to read the first pages of Proust's fiction, I had just opened the first tin of sardines that I had bought – a product of Portugal – and had emptied the contents over two slices of dry bread. Being hungry and anxious not to waste anything that had cost me money, I ate all of this meal while I read from the book propped open in front of me.

For an hour after I had eaten my meal, I felt a growing but still bearable discomfort. But as I read on, my stomach became more and more offended by what I had forced into it. At about the time when I was reading of how the narrator had tasted a mouthful of cake mixed with tea and had been overcome by an exquisite sensation, the taste of the dry bread mixed with the sardine oil was so strong in my mouth that I was overcome by nausea.

During the twenty or so years from 1961 until my paperback *Swann's Way* was enclosed in black plastic and stored above my ceiling, I would feel in my mind at least a mild flatulence whenever I handled the book, and I would see again in my mind, whenever I noticed the hint of gold in the brown, the light from the electric globe above me glinting in the film of oil left behind after I had rubbed my crusts around my dinner plate in my rented room in Malvern on a summer evening in 1961.

While I was writing the previous sentence, I saw in my mind an image of a bed of tall flowers near a stone wall which is the wall of a house on its shaded side.

I would like to be sure that the image of the tall flowers and the stone wall first appeared in my mind while I was reading *Swann's Way* in 1961, but I can be sure of no more than that I see those flowers and that wall in my mind whenever I try to remember myself first reading the prose fiction of Marcel Proust. I am not writing today about a book or even about my reading of a book. I am writing about images that appear in my mind whenever I try to remember my having read that book.

The image of the flowers is an image of the blooms of the Russell lupins that I saw in an illustration on a packet of seeds in 1948, when I was nine years old. I had asked my mother to buy the seeds because I wanted to make a flower-bed among the patches of dust and gravel and the clumps of spear grass around the rented weatherboard house at 244 Neale Street, Bendigo, which I used to see in my mind continually during the years from 1966 to 1971, while I was writing about the house at 42 Leslie Street, Bassett, in my book of fiction *Tamarisk Row*.

I planted the seeds in the spring of 1948. I watered the bed and tended the green plants that grew from the seeds. However, the spring of 1948 was the season when my father decided suddenly to move from Bendigo and when I was taken across the Great Divide and the Western Plains to a rented weatherboard cottage near the Southern Ocean in the district of Allansford before I could compare whatever flowers might have appeared on my plants with the coloured illustration on the packet of seeds.

While I was writing the previous paragraph, a further detail appeared in the image of the garden beside the wall in my mind. I now see in the garden in my mind an image of a small boy with dark hair. The boy is staring and listening. I understand today that the image of the boy would first have appeared in my mind at some time during the five months before January 1961 and soon after I had looked for the first time at a photograph taken in the year 1910 in the grounds of a State school near the Southern Ocean in the district of Allansford. The district of Allansford is the district where my father was born and where my father's parents lived for forty years until the death of my father's father in 1949 and where I spent my holidays as a child.

The photograph is of the pupils of the school assembled in rows beside a garden bed where the taller plants might be delphiniums or even Russell lupins. Among the smallest children in the front row, a dark-haired boy aged six years stares towards the camera and turns his head slightly as though afraid of missing some word or some signal from his elders and his betters. The staring and listening boy of 1910 became in time the man who became my father twenty-nine years after the photograph had been taken and who died in August 1960, two weeks before I looked for the first time at the photograph, which my father's mother had kept for fifty years in her collection of photographs, and five months before I read for the first time the volume *Swann's Way* in the paperback edition with the brownish cover.

During his lifetime my father read a number of books, but even if my father had been alive in January 1961, I would not have talked to him about *Swann's Way*. Whenever my father and I had talked about books during the last five years of his life, we had quarrelled. If my father had been alive in January 1961 and if he had seen me reading *Swann's Way*, he would have asked me first what sort of man the author was.

Whenever my father had asked me such a question in the five years before he died in 1960, I had answered him in the way that I thought would be most likely to annoy him. In January 1961, when I was reading *Swann's Way* for the first time, I knew hardly anything about the author. Since 1961, however, I have read two biographies of Marcel Proust, one by André Maurois and one by George D. Painter. Today, Monday 3 July 1989, I am able to compose the answer that would have been most likely to annoy my father if he had asked me his question in January 1961.

My father's question: What sort of man was the author of that book? My answer: The author of this book was an effeminate, hypochondriac Frenchman who mixed mostly with the upper classes, who spent most of his life indoors, and who was never obliged to work for his living.

My father is now annoyed, but he has a second question: What do I hope to gain from reading a book by such a man?

In order to answer this question truthfully, I would have to speak to my father about the thing that has always mattered most to me. I would never have spoken about this thing to my father during his lifetime, partly because I did not understand at that time what the thing is that has always mattered most to me and partly because I preferred not to speak to my father about things that mattered to me. However, I am going to answer my father truthfully today.

I believe today, Monday 3 July 1989, that the thing that has always mattered most to me is a place. Occasionally during my life I may have seemed to believe that I might arrive at this place by travelling to one or another district of the country in which I was born or even to some other country, but for most of my life I have supposed that the place that matters most to me is a place in my mind and that I ought to think not of myself arriving in the future at the place but of myself in the future seeing the place more clearly than I can see any other image in my mind and seeing also that all the other images that matter to me are arranged around that image of a place like an arrangement of townships on a map.

My father might be disappointed to learn that the place that matters most to me is a district of my mind rather than a district of the country where he and I were born, but he might be pleased to learn that I have often supposed that the place in my mind is grassy countryside with a few trees in the distance.

From the time when I first began as a child to read books of fiction, I looked forward to seeing places in my mind as a result of my reading. On a hot afternoon in January 1961, I read in *Swann's Way* a certain place-name. I remember today, Tuesday 4 July 1989, my feeling when I read that place-name more than twenty-eight years ago, something of the joy that the narrator of *Swann's Way* describes himself as having felt whenever he discovered part of the truth underlying the surface of his life. I will come back to that place-name later and by a different route.

If my father could tell me what mattered most to him during his lifetime, he would probably tell me about two dreams that he dreamed often during his lifetime. The first was a dream of himself owning a sheep or cattle property; the second was a dream of his winning regularly large sums of money from bookmakers at race meetings. My father might even tell me about a single dream that arose out of the other two dreams. This was a dream of his setting out one morning from his sheep or cattle property with his own racehorse and with a trusted friend and of his travelling a hundred miles and more to a racecourse on the edge of an unfamiliar town and there backing his horse with large sums of money and soon afterwards watching his horse win the race that he had been backed to win.

If I could ask my father whether the dreams that mattered to him were connected with any images that appeared in his mind as a result of his reading books of fiction, my father might remind me that he had once told me that his favourite book of fiction was a book by a South African writer, Stuart Cloete, about a farmer and his sons who drove their herds of cattle and flocks of sheep out of the settled districts of southern Africa and north-west into what seemed to them endless unclaimed grazing lands.

One of my feelings while I read certain pages of *Swann's Way* in January 1961, was a feeling that my father would have agreed with. I resented the characters' having so much leisure for talking about such things as painting and the architecture of churches.

Although January 1961 was part of my summer holidays, I was already preparing to teach a class of forty-eight primary-school children as from February and to study two subjects at university during my evenings. The characters in *Swann's Way* mostly seemed to lead idle lives or even to enjoy the earnings of inherited wealth. I would have liked to frogmarch the idle characters out of their salons and to confine them each to a room with only a sink and a gas ring and a few pieces of cheap furniture. I would then have enjoyed hearing the idlers calling in vain for their servants.

I heard myself jeering at the idlers. What? Not talking about the Dutch Masters, or about little churches in Normandy with something of the Persian about them?

Sometimes while I read the early pages of *Swann's Way* in 1961, and when I still thought the book was partly a fictional memoir, I took a strong dislike to the pampered boy who had been the narrator as a child. I saw myself dragging him out of the arms of his mother and away from his aunts and his grandmother and then thrusting him into the backyard of the tumbledown farm-workers' cottage where my family lived after we had left Bendigo, putting an axe into his hand, pointing out to him one of the heaps of timber that I had split into kindling wood for the kitchen stove, and then hearing the namby-pamby bleating for his mama.

In 1961, whenever I heard in my mind the adult characters of *Swann's Way* talking about art or literature or architecture I heard them talking in the language used by the gentlemen and lady members of the Metropolitan Golf Club in North Road, Oakleigh, where I had worked as a caddy and an assistant barman from 1954 to 1956.

In the 1950s, there were still people in Melbourne who seemed to want you to believe that they had been born or educated in England or that they had visited England often or that they thought and behaved as English people did. These people in Melbourne spoke with what I would call a world-weary drawl. I heard that drawl by day from men in plus-four trousers while I trudged behind them down fairways on Saturday and Sunday afternoons. In the evenings of those days, I heard the same drawl in the bar of the golf club where the same men, now dressed in slacks and blazers, drank Scotch whisky or gin-and-tonic.

One day soon after I had first begun working at the Metropolitan Golf Club, I looked into a telephone directory for the addresses of some of the most outrageous drawlers. I found not only that most of them lived in the suburb of Toorak, but that most of this majority lived in the same neighbourhood, which consisted of St Georges Road, Lansell Road, and a few adjoining streets.

Six years after I learned this, and only a few months before I first read *Swann's Way*, I travelled a little out of my way one afternoon between the city and Malvern. On that fine spring afternoon, I looked from a window of a tram down each of St Georges Road and Lansell Road, Toorak. I got an impression of tall, pale-coloured houses surrounded by walled gardens in which the trees were just coming into flower.

While I read *Swann's Way* in 1961, any reference to Paris caused me to see in my mind the pale-coloured walls and mansions of St Georges Road and Lansell Road. When I first read the word *faubourg*, which I had never previously read but the meaning of which I guessed, I saw the upper half of a prunus tree appearing from behind a tall wall of cream-coloured stone. The first syllable of the word *faubourg* was linked with the abundant frothiness of the pink flowers on the tree, while the second syllable suggested the solid, forbidding wall. If I read a reference to some public garden or some woods in Paris, I saw in my mind the landscape that I connected with the world-weary drawlers of Melbourne: the view through the plate-glass windows of the dining room and bar in the clubhouse of the Metropolitan Golf Club – the view of the undulating, velvety eighteenth green and the close-mown fairway of cushiony couch grass reaching back between stands of gum trees and wattle trees to the point where the trees almost converged behind the eighteenth tee, leaving a gap past which the hazy seventeenth fairway formed the further part of the twofold vista.

My father despised the drawlers of Melbourne, and if ever he had read about such a character as Monsieur Swann, my father would have despised him also as a drawler. I found myself, at the Metropolitan Golf Club in the 1950s, wanting to distinguish between the drawlers that I could readily despise and a sort of drawler that I was ready to respect, if only I could have learned certain things about him.

The drawlers that I could readily despise were such as the grey-haired man that I heard one day drawling his opinion of an American film or play that he had seen recently. The man lived in one of the two roads that I named earlier and was wealthy as a result of events that had happened before his birth in places far from the two roads. The chief of these events were the man's great-grandfather's having brewed and then peddled on the goldfields of Victoria in the 1860s an impressively named but probably ineffective patent medicine.

The American film or play that the drawler had seen was named *The Moon Is Blue*. I had learned previously from news-papers that some people in Melbourne had wanted *The Moon Is Blue* to be banned, as many films and plays and books were banned in Melbourne in the 1950s. The people had wanted it banned because it was said to contain jokes with double meanings.

The drawler had said to three other men, while the four were walking among the complex arrangement of vistas of green fairways that I would later see in my mind from 1961 onwards whenever I would read in one or another volume of *À la recherche du temps perdu* the name of one or another wood or park in Paris, 'I've never laughed so much in my whole life. It was absolutely the funniest show I've ever seen!'

On the afternoon nearly forty years ago when I heard the grey-haired drawler drawl those words, I readily despised him because I was disappointed to learn that a man who had inherited a fortune and who might have taken his pleasure from the ownership of a vast library or a stable of racehorses could boast of having sniggered at what my school-friends and I would have called dirty jokes.

Six or seven years later, when I read for the first time about Swann, the descendant of stockbrokers, and his passion for Odette de Crecy, I saw that the Swann in my mind had the grey hair and wore the plus-four trousers of the great-grandson of the brewer and peddler of patent medicines.

The Swann in my mind was not usually one of the *despised* drawlers. Sometimes at the Metropolitan Golf Club, but more often when I looked at the owners of racehorses in the mounting-yard of one or another racecourse, I saw a sort of drawler that I admired. This drawler might have lived for some time during each year behind a walled garden in Melbourne, but at other times he lived surrounded by the land that had been since the years before the discovery of gold in Victoria the source of his family's wealth and standing – he lived on his sheep or cattle property.

In my seventh book of fiction, *O, Dem Golden Slippers*, which I expect to be published during 1993, I will explain something of what has happened in the mind of a person such as myself whenever he has happened to see in the mounting yard of a racecourse in any of the towns or cities of Victoria an owner of a racehorse who is also the owner of a sheep or cattle property far from that town or city. Here I have time only to explain first that for most of my life I have seen most of the sheep or cattle properties in my mind as lying in the district of Victoria in my mind that is sometimes called the Western Plains. When I look towards that district in my mind while I write these words, I look towards the north-west of my mind. However, when I used to stand on the Warrnambool racecourse during my summer holidays in the 1950s, which is to say, when I stood in those days at a point nearly three hundred kilometres south-west of where I sit at this moment, I still saw often in the north-west of my mind sheep or cattle properties far from where I stood, and doubly far from where I sit today writing these words.

Today, 26 July 1989, I looked at a map of the southern part of Africa. I wanted to verify that the districts where the chief character in my father's favourite book of fiction arrived with his flocks and herds at what might be called his sheep or cattle property would have been in fact north-west of the settled districts. After having looked at the map, I now believe that the owner of the flocks and herds was more likely to have travelled north-east. That being so, when my father said that the man in southern Africa had travelled north-west in order to discover the site of his sheep or cattle property, my father perhaps had in mind that the whole of Africa was north-west of the suburb of Oakleigh South, where my father and I lived at the time when he told me about his favourite book of fiction, so that anyone travelling in any direction in Africa was travelling towards a place north-west of my father and myself, and any character in a book of fiction who was described as having travelled in any direction in Africa would have seemed to my father to have travelled towards a place in the north-west of my father's mind. Or, my father, who was born and who lived for much of his life in the south-east of Australia, may have seen all desirable places in his mind as lying in the north-west of his mind.

Before I mentioned just now the map of the southern part of Africa, I was about to mention the second of two things connected with my seeing on racecourses the owners of distant sheep or cattle properties. I was about to mention the first of those owners that I can recall having seen. The owner and his horse and the trainer of his horse had come to the summer meeting at Warrnambool, in one of the early years of the 1950s, from the district around Apsley. At that time I had seen one photograph of the district around Apsley: a coloured photograph on the cover of the *Leader*, which was once the chief rival of the *Weekly Times* for the readership of persons in rural Victoria. The photograph showed grassy countryside with a few trees in the distance. Something in the colours of the photograph had caused me to remember it afterwards as having been taken during the late afternoon.

The only map that I owned in the 1950s was a road map of Victoria. When I looked at that map, I saw that Apsley was the furthest west of any town in the Western District of Victoria. Past Apsley was only a pale no-man's-land – the first few miles of South Australia – and then the end of the map.

The man from the district around Apsley stood out among the owners in the mounting-yard. He wore a pale-grey suit and a pale-grey hat with green and blue feathers in the band. Under the rear brim of his hat, his silvery hair was bunched in a style very different from the cropped style of the men around him. As soon as I had seen the man from the district around Apsley, I had heard him in my mind speaking in a world-weary drawl but I was far from despising him.

I have always become alert whenever I have read in a book of fiction a reference to a character's country estates. The ownership of a country estate has always seemed to me to add a further layer to a person: to suggest, as it were, far-reaching vistas within the person. 'You see me here, among these walls of pale stone topped by pink blossoms,' I hear the person saying, 'and you think of the places in my mind as being only the streets of this suburb – or this *faubourg*. You have not seen yet, at a further place in my mind, the leafy avenue leading to the circular driveway surrounding the vast lawn; the mansion whose upper windows overlook grassy countryside with a few trees in the distance, or a stream that is marked on certain mornings and evenings by strands of mist.'

I read in *Swann's Way* during January 1961 that Swann was the owner of a park and a country house along one of the two ways where the narrator and his parents went walking on Sundays. According to my memory, I learned at first that Swann's park was bounded on one side at least by a white fence behind which grew numerous lilacs of both the white-flowering and the mauve-flowering varieties. Before I had read about that park and those lilacs, I had seen Swann in my mind as the drawler in plus-four trousers that I described earlier. After I had read about the white fence and the white and lilac-coloured flowers, I saw in my mind a different Swann.

As anyone who has read my first book of fiction, *Tamarisk Row*, will know, the chief character of that book builds his first racecourse and first sees in his mind the district of Tamarisk Row while he kneels in the dirt under a lilac tree. As anyone will know who has read the piece 'First Love' in my sixth book of fiction, *Velvet Waters*, the chief character of 'First Love' decides, after many years of speculating about the matter, that his racing colours are lilac and brown. After I had first read about the park and the lilacs at Combray, I remembered having read earlier in *Swann's Way* that Swann was a good friend of the Prince of Wales and a member of the Jockey Club. After I had remembered this, I saw Swann in my mind as having the suit and the hat and the bunched silver hair beneath the brim of his hat of the man from Apsley, far to the north-west of Warrnambool. I decided that Swann's racing colours would have been a combination of white and lilac. In 1961 when I decided this, the only set of white and lilac colours that I had seen had been carried by a horse named Parentive, owned and trained by a Mr A.C. Gartner. I noticed today what I believe I had not previously noticed: although the one occasion when I saw the horse Parentive race was a Saturday at Caulfield racecourse at some time during the late 1950s, Mr Gartner and his horse came from Hamilton, which of course, is north-west from where I sit now and on the way to Apsley.

One detail of my image of Monsieur Swann, the owner of racehorses, changed a few months later. In July 1961, I became the owner of a small book illustrated with reproductions of some of the works of the French artist Raoul Dufy. After I had seen the gentlemen in the mounting-yards of the racecourses in those illustrations, I saw above the bunched silvery hair of Monsieur Swann in my mind not a grey hat with blue and green feathers but a black top hat.

I first read the first of the twelve volumes of the 1969 Chatto and Windus edition of *À la recherche du temps perdu*, as I wrote earlier, in the late summer and the autumn of 1973, when I was thirty-four years of age. On a hot morning while I was still reading the first volume, I was lying with the book beside me on a patch of grass in my backyard in a north-eastern suburb of Melbourne. While my eyes were closed for a moment against the glare of the sun, I heard the buzzing of a large fly in the grass near my ear.

Somewhere in *À la recherche du temps perdu*, I seem to remember, is a short passage about the buzzing of flies on warm mornings, but even if that passage is in the part of the text that I had read in 1961, I did not recall my having previously read about the buzzing of flies in Marcel Proust's texts when the large fly buzzed in the grass near my ear in the late summer of 1973. What I recalled at that moment was one of those parcels of a few moments of seemingly lost time that the narrator of *À la recherche du temps perdu* warns us never deliberately to go in search of. The parcel came to me, of course, not as a quantity of something called time, whatever that may be, but as a knot of feelings and sensations that I had long before experienced and had not since recalled.

The sensations that had been suddenly restored to me were those that I had experienced as a boy of fifteen years walking alone in the spacious garden of the house belonging to the widowed mother of my father in the city of Warrnambool in the south-west of Victoria on a Saturday morning of my summer holidays. The feelings that had been suddenly restored to me were feelings of expectancy and joy. On the Saturday morning in January 1954, I had heard the buzzing of a large fly while I had been looking at a bush of tiger lilies in bloom.

As I write this on 28 July 1989, I notice for the first time that the colour of the tiger lilies in my mind resembles the colour of the cover of the biography of Marcel Proust by André Maurois that I quoted from in my fifth book of fiction, *Inland*. The passage that I quoted from in that book includes the phrase *invisible yet enduring lilacs*, and I have just now understood that that phrase ought to be the title of this piece of writing . . . *Invisible Yet Enduring Lilacs*.

My book *Inland* includes a passage about tiger-lilies that I wrote while I saw in my mind the blooms on the bush of tiger lilies that I was looking at when I heard the large fly buzzing in January 1954.

I had felt expectancy and joy on the Saturday morning in January 1954 because I was going to go later on that day to the so-called summer meeting at Warrnambool racecourse. Although I was already in love with horse-racing, I was still a schoolboy and seldom had the money or the time for going to race meetings. On that Saturday morning, I had never previously been to a race meeting at Warrnambool. The buzzing of the fly was connected in my mind with the heat of the afternoon to come and with the dust and the dung in the saddling paddock. I had felt a particular expectancy and joy on that morning while I had pronounced to myself the name *tiger lily* and while I had stared at the colours of the blooms on the bush. The names of the racehorses of the Western District of Victoria and the racing colours of their owners were mostly unknown to me in 1954. On that Saturday morning, I was trying to see in my mind the colours, unfamiliar and striking, carried by some horse that had been brought to Warrnambool from a hundred miles away in the north-west, and I was trying to hear in my mind the name of that horse.

During the morning in the late summer of 1973 when I heard the buzzing of the large fly soon after I had begun to read the first of the twelve volumes of *À la recherche du temps perdu*, the feelings that came back to me from the Saturday morning nineteen years before only added to the feelings of expectancy and joy that I had already felt as I had prepared to read the twelve volumes. On that morning in my backyard in 1973, I had been aware for twelve years that one of the important place-names in *À la recherche du temps perdu* had the power to bring to my mind details of a place such as I had wanted to see in my mind during most of my life. That place was a country estate in my mind. The owner of the estate spent his mornings in his library, where the windows overlooked grassy countryside with a few trees in the distance, and his afternoons exercising his racehorses. Once each week, he travelled a hundred miles and more with one of his horses and with his distinctive silk racing colours south-east to a race meeting.

At some time during 1949, several years before I had attended any race-meeting or had heard the name of Marcel Proust, my father told me that he had carved his name at two places in the sandstone that underlies the district of Allansford where he was born and where his remains have lain buried since 1960. The first of the two places was a pinnacle of rock standing high out of the water in the bay known as Childers Cove. My father told me in 1949 that he had once swum through the fifty yards of turbulent water between the shore and Steeple Rock with a tomahawk tied to his body and had carved his name and the date on the side of Steeple Rock that faced the Southern Ocean. The second of the two places was the wall of a quarry on a hill overlooking the bays of the Southern Ocean known as Stanhopes' Bay, Sandy Bay, and Murnane's Bay, just south-east of Childers Cove.

During the first twenty-five years after my father had died, I thought about neither of the two places where he had once carved his name. Then, in 1985, twenty-five years after my father had died, and while I was writing a piece of fiction about a man who had read a story about a man who thought often about the bedrock far beneath his feet, an image of a stone quarry came into my mind and I wrote that the father of the narrator of the story had carved his name on the wall of a quarry, and I gave the title 'Stone Quarry' to my piece of fiction, which until then had lacked a title.

At some time during the spring of 1985 and while I was still writing 'Stone Quarry', I received through the post a page of the *Warrnambool Standard* illustrated by two reproductions of photographs. The first of the two photographs was of Childers Cove as it had appeared for as long as European persons had looked at it, with Steeple Rock standing out of the water fifty metres from shore and the Southern Ocean in the background. The second photograph showed Childers Cove as it has appeared since the day or the night in 1985 when waves of the Southern Ocean caused Steeple Rock to topple and the surfaces of sandstone where my father had carved his name to sink beneath the water.

In the autumn of 1989, while I was making notes for this piece of writing but before I had thought of mentioning my father in the writing, a man who was about to travel with a camera from Melbourne to the district of Allansford offered to bring back to me photographs of any places that I might wish to see in photographs.

I gave the man directions for finding the quarry on the hill overlooking the Southern Ocean and asked him to look on the walls of the quarry for the inscription that my father had told me forty years before that he had carved.

Two days ago, on 28 July 1989, while I was writing the earlier passage that has to do with the buzzing of a fly near a bush of tiger lilies at Warrnambool in 1954, I found among the mail that had just arrived at my house a coloured photograph of an area of sandstone in which four letters and four numerals are visible. The four numerals 1-9-2-1 allow me to believe that my father stood in front of the area of sandstone in the year 1921, when he was aged seventeen years and when

Marcel Proust was aged fifty years, as I am today, and had one year of his life remaining. The four letters allow me to believe that my father in 1921 carved in the sandstone the first letter of the first of his given names followed by all the letters of his surname but that rainwater running down the wall of the quarry caused part of the sandstone to break off and to fall away at some time during the sixty-eight years between 1921 and 1989, leaving only the letter *R* for *Reginald* followed by the first three letters of my father's and my surname.

I have a number of photographs of myself standing in one or another garden and in front of one or another wall, but the earliest of these photographs shows me standing, in the year 1940, on a patch of grass in front of a wall of sandstone that is part of a house on its sunlit side. The wall that I mentioned earlier – the wall that appears as an image in my mind together with the image of a small boy and the image of a bed of tall flowers whenever I try to imagine myself first reading the first pages of *À la recherche du temps perdu* – is not the same wall that appears in bright sunlight in the photograph of myself in 1940. The wall in my mind is a wall of the same house that I stood beside on a day of sunshine in 1940, but the wall in my mind is a wall on the shaded side of the house. (I have already explained that the image of the boy in my mind is an image of a boy who was first photographed thirty years before the day of sunshine in 1940.)

The house with the walls of sandstone was built by my father's father less than one kilometre from where the Southern Ocean forms the bay known as Sandy Bay, which is next to the bays known as Murnane's Bay and Childers Cove on the south-west coast of Victoria. All the walls of the house were quarried from the place where the surname of the boy who appears in my mind as listening and staring whenever I remember myself first reading about Combray now appears as no more than the letters MUR . . . the root in the Latin language, the language of my father's religion, of the word for *wall*.

At the summer race meeting at Warrnambool racecourse in January 1960, which was the last summer meeting before the death of my father and the second-last summer meeting before my first reading the first part of *À la recherche du temps perdu*, I read in my racebook the name of a racehorse from far to the north-west of Warrnambool. The name was a place-name consisting of two words. The first of the two was a word that I had never previously read but a word that I supposed was from the French language. The second word was the word *Bay*. The colours to be worn by the rider of the horse were brown and white stripes.

I found the name and the colours of the horse peculiarly attractive. During the afternoon, I looked forward to seeing the owner of the horse and his colours in the mounting-yard. However, when the field was announced for the race in which the horse had been entered, I learned that the horse had been scratched.

During the twelve months following that race meeting, I often pronounced in my mind the name of the racehorse with the name ending in the word *Bay*. During the same time, I often saw in my mind the brown and white colours carried by the horse. During the same time also, I saw in my mind images of a sheep or cattle property in the far west of Victoria in my mind (that is, north-west of the south-west of Victoria in my mind) and of the owner of the property, who lived in a house with a vast library. However, none of the images of the sheep or cattle property or of the owner of the property or of his vast library has appeared in my mind since January

1961, when I read in *Swann's Way* the first of the two words of the horse's name.

In January 1961, I learned from the paperback volume with the title *Swann's Way* that the word that I had previously known only as part of the name of a racehorse that had been entered in a race at Warrnambool racecourse, as though its owner and its trainer were going to bring the horse out of the north-west in the same way that the horse had been brought in the dream that had mattered most to my father, was the name of one of the places that mattered most to the narrator of *Swann's Way* from among the places around Combray, where he spent his holidays in each year of his childhood.

After I had learned this, I saw in my mind whenever I said to myself the name of the horse that had not arrived at Warrnambool racecourse from the north-west, or whenever I saw in my mind a silk jacket with brown and white stripes, a stream flowing through grassy countryside with trees in the background. I saw the stream at one point flowing past a quiet reach that I called in my mind a bay

A bay in a stream might have seemed a geographical absurdity, but I saw in my mind the calm water, the green rushes, the green grass in the fields behind the rushes. I saw in the green fields in my mind the white fence topped by the white and lilac flowers of the lilac bushes on the estate of the man with the bunched silvery hair who had named one of his racehorses after a geographical absurdity or a proper noun in the works of Marcel Proust. I saw, at the place named Apsley in my mind, far to the north-west of Warrnambool in my mind, enduring lilacs that had previously been invisible.

At some time during the seven years since I last read the whole of *À la recherche du temps perdu*, I looked into my *Times*

Atlas of the World and learned that the racehorse whose name I had read in the racebook at Warrnambool twelve months before I first read *Swann's Way* had almost certainly not been named after any geographical feature in France or after any word in the works of Marcel Proust but had almost certainly been named after a bay on the south coast of Kangaroo Island, off the coast of South Australia.

Since my having learned that the horse that failed to arrive from the north-west at Warrnambool racecourse in the last summer of my father's life and the last summer before I first read the fiction of Marcel Proust was almost certainly named after a bay on Kangaroo Island, I have sometimes seen in my mind, soon after I have pronounced in my mind the name of the horse or soon after I have seen in my mind a silk jacket with brown and white stripes, waves of the Southern Ocean rolling from far away in the direction of South Africa, rolling past Kangaroo Island towards the south-west coast of Victoria, and breaking against the base of Steeple Rock in Childers Cove, near Murnane's Bay, and causing Steeple Rock at last to topple. I have sometimes seen in my mind, soon after Steeple Rock has toppled in my mind, a wall of a stone house and near the wall a small boy who will later, as a young man, choose for his colours lilac from the white and lilac colours of the Monsieur Swann in his mind and brown from the white and brown colours of the racehorse in his mind from far to the north-west of Warrnambool: the racehorse whose name he will read for the first time in a racebook in the last summer before he reads for the first time a book of fiction with the title *Swann's Way*. And I have sometimes seen in my mind, soon after I have seen in my mind the things just mentioned, one or another detail of a place in my mind where I see together things that I might have expected to lie for ever far apart;

where rows of lilacs appear on a sheep or cattle property; where my father, who had never heard the name *Marcel Proust*, is the narrator of an immense and intricately patterned work of fiction; where a racehorse has for its name the word *Bay* preceded by the word *Vivonne*.

(*TENSION*, NO. 21, JUNE 1990)

STREAM SYSTEM

This morning, in order to reach the place where I am now, I went a little out of my way. I took the shortest route from my house to the place that you people probably know as SOUTH ENTRY. That is to say, I walked from the front gate of my house due west and downhill to Salt Creek then uphill and still due west from Salt Creek to the watershed between Salt Creek and a nameless creek that runs into Darebin Creek. When I reached the high ground that drains into the nameless creek, I walked north-west until I was standing about thirty metres south-east of the place that is denoted on Page 66A of Edition 18 of the Melway Street Directory of Greater Melbourne by the words STREAM SYSTEM.

I could hardly doubt that I was looking at the place that was denoted in my map by the words STREAM SYSTEM. Yet I was looking at two bodies of yellow-brown water, each of which seemed roughly oval. When I had looked a few days before at the words STREAM SYSTEM, each of those words had been printed on one of two bodies of pale blue, each with a distinctive outline.

'Stream System' was written to be read aloud at a gathering in the Department of English at La Trobe University in 1988.

The body of pale blue on which the word STREAM had been printed had the outline of a human heart that had been twisted slightly from its usual shape. When I had first noticed this outline on the map, I asked myself why I had thought of a human heart twisted slightly when I ought to have been thinking of a body of yellow-brown water of a roughly oval shape. I recalled that I had never seen a human heart either twisted slightly or occupying its usual shape. The thing that I had seen that was nearest in shape to the slightly twisted heart was a certain tapering outline that was part of a line drawing of an item of gold jewellery in a catalogue issued by the Direct Supply Jewellery Company Pty Ltd in about the year 1946.

My father had five sisters. Of those five women, only one married. The other four women lived for most of their lives in the house where they had been children. In the years when I first knew my father's unmarried sisters, who were, of course, my aunts, they kept mostly to their house. However, my aunts subscribed to many newspapers and periodicals and they wrote away, as they called it, for many mail-order catalogues. During one of the summer holidays that I spent during the 1940s in the house where my aunts lived, I used to sit for perhaps a half-hour every day in the bed-sitting room of one of my aunts, looking through the hundred and more pages of the catalogue of the Direct Supply Jewellery Company.

The only gold object that I had seen when I first looked through the catalogue had been the thin wedding ring that my mother wore, but I did not consider my mother's ring the equal of any of the items in the pages that I looked at. I questioned my aunt about the many jewels that I had never seen:

the gentlemen's cuff-links and signet rings. I asked especially about the ladies' rings and bracelets and pendants.

When I wanted to see in my mind the men and women who wore the jewels that I had never seen, I thought of the illustrations in the *Saturday Evening Post*, which my aunts subscribed to. The men and women in those illustrations were the men and women of America: the men and women that I saw going about their business whenever I looked away from the main characters in the foreground of an American film.

When I asked myself whether I would one day handle or even wear on my own body the jewels that I had never seen, I seemed to be asking myself whether I would one day live among the men and women of America in places far back from the main characters in American films. When I asked myself this question I seemed to be trying to see America from where I sat. When I tried to see America from where I sat, I seemed to be looking across seemingly endless grasslands.

When I sat in the cane chair in my aunt's room, I faced north. By turning my body a little in the chair I was able to face north-east, which seemed to me the direction of America. If the stone walls of the house around me had been lifted away, I could have looked north-east for half a mile across yellow-brown grass towards a slight ridge known as Lawlers' Hill. I could have seen beyond Lawlers' Hill only pale-blue sky, but if, while I sat in my chair, I could have thought of myself as standing on Lawlers' Hill and looking north-east, I would have seen in my mind yellow-brown grass reaching a mile and more north-east towards the next slight hill.

If I had wanted to think of myself as standing at the highest point that I could have reached if I had walked in any direction from my aunts' house, I would have thought of what lay behind me while I sat in my aunt's chair.

Behind the stone walls of the house was a paddock known as the Rye Paddock, which was about a quarter of a mile across. The fence at the far side of the Rye Paddock was a barbed-wire fence looking no different from the hundreds of barbed-wire fences in the district around. But that fence was a notable fence; that fence was part of the southern boundary of all the farms on the mainland of Australia.

On the far side of that fence the land rose. The land rose more steeply as it reached further south. The more steeply the land rose and the further south it reached, the less the land was covered by yellow-brown grass, but whenever I had walked on the rising land I had noticed yellow-brown grass still growing in tussocks, and I understood that I was still standing on a grassland.

About three hundred yards south of the southern boundary of the farm where I sat often with my face to the north or the north-east, the land rose to the highest point that I could have reached if I had walked in any direction from my aunts' house. At that point the land ended. Whenever I looked at that point I saw that the land had a mind to go on rising and to go on reaching south. I saw too that the grass had a mind to grow on the land for as far as the land might rise and for as far as the land might reach to the south. But at that point the land ended. Beyond that point was only pale-blue sky, and beneath the pale-blue sky was only water – the dark-blue water of the Southern Ocean.

If, while I was sitting in my aunt's room, I had thought of myself as standing at the high point where the land ended and as looking towards America, even then I would have thought of myself as seeing to the north-east only seemingly endless yellow-brown grass. If, while I was sitting in my aunt's room, I had wanted to think of myself as seeing more than seemingly endless grass, I would have had to think of myself as standing at some impossible vantage-point. If I could have thought of myself as standing at such a vantage-point, I would have thought of myself as seeing not only seemingly endless yellow-brown grass and seemingly pale-blue sky but dark-blue water on the other side of the yellow-brown grass and, on the far side of the dark-blue water, the yellow-brown and endless grasslands under the pale-blue and endless sky of America.

When I asked my aunt where I might see some of the pieces of jewellery illustrated in the catalogue, she told me that her married sister was the owner of a pendant. The pendant had been a wedding present to my one married aunt from her husband.

My married aunt and her husband lived at that time about four miles north-east across the yellow-brown grass. My aunt and her husband sometimes visited the four unmarried sisters. After I had heard about the pendant, I tried often to see in my mind what I expected to see one day below the throat of my father's sister in the same house where I had sat turning pages of illustrations of jewellery. I saw in my mind a gold chain and hanging from the gold chain a gold heart.

As a child I tried often to see myself as a man and to see the place where I would live after I had become a man. Often while I looked into the jewellery catalogue I would try to see myself as a man wearing cuff-links and signet rings. Often while I turned the pages of the *Saturday Evening Post* I would try to see myself as a man living in a place that was like a landscape in America.

I was never able to see myself as a man, but I was sometimes able to hear in my mind some of the words that I would speak as a man. I was sometimes able to hear in my mind the words that I would speak as a man to the young woman who was about to become my wife. And sometimes I was able even to hear what the young woman would speak to me from close beside me.

After I had been told about my aunt's pendant, I sometimes heard the following words as though they were spoken by myself as a man. *Here is your wedding present, darling.* And I sometimes heard the following words as though they were spoken by the young woman who was about to become my wife. *Oh! A pendant with a gold heart. Thank you, darling.*

When I had looked at the body of pale blue on which the word SYSTEM had been printed, I had seen in my mind the outline of a pair of female lips boldly marked with lipstick.

When I first saw such an outline of lips I was sitting in a dark cinema with my mother and my only brother, who was younger than myself. The cinema may have been the Circle in Preston or it may have been the Lyric or the Plaza or the Princess in Bendigo. The lips were on the face of a young woman who was about to kiss the man who was about to become her husband.

When I first saw such an outline of lips I had been watching the young woman so that I could afterwards see her in my mind. I wanted to think of her as the young woman who would become my wife when I had become a man. But when I had seen from the shape of her lips that the young woman was about to be kissed, then I had turned my head and had looked away from the main characters in the foreground. I had looked away because I remembered that I was sitting beside my mother and my brother.

In my aunt's room, trying to see in my mind myself as a man giving a pendant as a wedding present, I sometimes saw in my mind the outline of the lips of the young woman who was about to become my wife. But as soon as I saw from the shape of the lips that the young woman was about to be kissed, I looked away from the foreground of my mind. I looked away because I remembered that I was sitting near my aunt and that the other three of my aunts were in their rooms nearby.

When I had looked at the outline of the body of pale blue that consisted of the body labelled STREAM and the body labelled SYSTEM and the narrow body of pale blue connecting the two – that is to say, when I had looked at the two larger bodies and the one smaller body that together comprised the body of pale blue labelled STREAM SYSTEM, I had noticed that the outline of the whole body brought to my mind a drooping moustache.

The first drooping moustache that I saw was the moustache of the man who was the father of my father and also of my father's five sisters, four of whom remained unmarried. My father's father was born in 1870 near the southern boundary of all the farms on the mainland of Australia. He was the son of an English mother and an Irish father. His Irish father had come to Australia from Ireland in about 1850. My father's father died in 1949, about three years after I had looked at the jewellery catalogue in his house. He would have been in the house while I turned the pages of the catalogue and while I thought of myself as a man giving a wedding present to a young woman, but he would not have seen me where I sat. He might have walked past the door of the room, but even then he would not have seen me turning the pages of the catalogue, because my chair would have been to one side of the doorway. I preferred to sit in places where my father's father was not likely to see me.

Whenever I have wondered why four of my father's five sisters remained unmarried, I have seen in my mind one or another of the four women sitting in her room and turning the pages of a jewellery catalogue or of a copy of the *Saturday Evening Post*. I have then seen in my mind my father's father walking to the door of the woman's room and the woman turning her head and looking away from what she had been about to look at.

But the drooping moustache of my father's father is not the only drooping moustache that I see in my mind when I look at the body of pale blue with STREAM printed on it and at the body of pale blue with SYSTEM printed on it and at the narrow body of pale blue connecting the two. I see in my mind also the drooping moustache of a man that I saw only once in my life, in about the year 1943. If the man had been still standing this morning where I saw him one afternoon in about the year 1943, I would have seen him this morning when I stood south-east of the yellow-brown water that was denoted by the body of pale blue and by the words STREAM SYSTEM in my map. I would have seen the man this morning because he would have been standing on the opposite side of the yellow-brown water from where I stood.

When I last saw the man with the drooping moustache, which was about forty-five years ago and near the place where I stood this morning, neither the man nor I nor any of the male persons around us saw a body of water either yellow-brown or pale blue in the place denoted by the words STREAM SYSTEM in the map of 1988. What we saw in that place was swampy ground overgrown by blackberries and with muddy drains leading into it. The drains ran downhill into the swampy ground from a shabby building of timber.

When I last saw the man with the drooping moustache in about the year 1943, he was standing near the shabby building of timber. The man was giving orders to a group of black-and-white fox terrier dogs and also to a group of men. Of the group of men receiving orders, three men were known to me by name. One was my father, one was a man known to me as Fat Collins, and the third was a young man known to me as Boy Webster.

I was allowed to watch the man giving orders to the dogs and the men, but I had been warned by my father to stand at a distance. Some of the men held in their hands hoses spouting water and some men held sticks for killing rats. The men with the hoses sent the water into holes under the shabby building. The men with sticks and the fox terrier dogs stood waiting for the rats to stagger out of their holes under the shabby building. Then the men with sticks would beat the rats and the fox terrier dogs would fasten their teeth in the necks of the rats. The man with the drooping moustache, who was the owner of the fox terrier dogs, shouted often at the men with the sticks to warn them against beating the dogs instead of the rats. The man had to shout often at the men with sticks because Fat Collins and Boy Webster and others of the men were by legal definition not in full possession of their minds.

The shabby building with rats living in holes beneath it was a pigsty where about fifty pigs lived in small muddy pens. The liquids that drained from the pigsty downhill into the swampy ground that lay in 1943 in the place denoted by the words STREAM SYSTEM were partly composed of leavings from the troughs where the pigs ate. The food that was put into the troughs for the pigs to eat was partly composed of leavings from the tables where the hundreds of men and women ate in the wards of Mont Park Hospital on the high ground north-east of the swamp and the pigsty. Of the men who stood around the pigsty on the day that I remember, all except my father and the man with the drooping moustache lived at Mont Park Hospital. My father spoke of the men as *patients* and warned me to speak of them only by that name. My mother sometimes called the men, out of my father's hearing, *loonies*.

The man with the drooping moustache gave orders to the patients only on that one day when he came to drive the rats from the pigsty. My father gave orders to the patients every day from mid-1941 to the end of 1943. During those years my father was the assistant manager of the farm that was part of the Mont Park Hospital for forty years until the cowyards and the haysheds and the pigsty and all the other shabby buildings were knocked down and a university was built in their place.

When no more rats seemed likely to come out from under the pigsty, Fat Collins and Boy Webster and the other patients began to aim the jets of water from their hoses at the dead rats lying on the grass. The patients seemed to want to send the dead rats sliding over the wet grass and downhill into the swampy ground. My father ordered the patients to turn off their hoses. I thought that he did this because he did not want the bodies of the rats to reach the swampy ground, but in fact my father only wanted to keep the men from wasting time. When the hoses had been turned off, my father ordered the patients to collect the dead rats in kerosene tins. The patients picked up the dead rats in their hands and carried the rats in kerosene tins down the slope that leads today to the yellow-brown water denoted by the pale blue in my map.

*

The outline of the bodies of pale blue resembles not only the moustache of my father's father and the moustache of the owner of the fox terrier dogs. Sometimes when I look at the outline of the body of pale blue that comprises the bodies labelled STREAM and SYSTEM and the narrow body connecting them and also the two small bodies at either side, I see in my mind the item of women's underclothing which is called by many people nowadays a bra but which I called during the 1940s and for some years afterwards a brassiere.

On my way this morning from my front gate to the place where I am now, I went, as I said before, a little out of my way. I followed a roundabout route.

After I had stood for a few moments south-east of the place that I am going to call from now on STREAM SYSTEM, I walked across the bridge between the two largest bodies of water. I walked, that is, between STREAM and SYSTEM. Or I walked, if you like, across the narrow connecting part between the two cup-shaped parts of a pale-blue (or yellow-brown) brassiere (or bra).

I kept on walking roughly north-west up the sloping land that had been forty-five years ago the wet grass where Fat Collins and Boy Webster and the other men had aimed their jets of water at the dead rats. I walked across yards where rows of motor cars stood and past the place that you people know as NORTH ENTRY.

Just short of Plenty Road I stopped. I turned and faced roughly south-west. I looked across what is now Kingsbury Drive at the house of red bricks on the south-eastern corner of the intersection of Kingsbury Drive and Plenty Road. I looked at the first window east of the north-eastern corner of the house, and I remembered a night in about 1943 when I had sat in the room behind that window. I remembered a night when I had sat with my arm around the shoulders of my brother while I tried to teach him what a brassiere was used for.

The building that I was looking at is no longer used as a house, but that building is the first house that I remember having lived in. I lived in that building of red bricks with my parents and my brother from mid-1941 until the end of 1943, when I was aged between two and four years.

On the night in about 1943 that I remembered this morning, I had found on a page of a newspaper a photograph of a young woman wearing what I thought was a brassiere. I had sat beside my young brother and put my arm around his shoulders. I had pointed to what I thought was the brassiere and then to the bare chest of the young woman.

I believe today, and I may even have believed in 1943, that my brother understood very little of what I told him. But I believed I had seen for the first time an illustration of a brassiere, and my brother was the only person I could talk to at that time.

I was talking to my brother about the brassiere when my father came into my room. My father had heard from outside the room what I had been saying to my brother and he had seen from the doorway of the room the illustration that I had been showing to my brother.

My father sat in the chair where I had been sitting with my brother. My father lifted me onto one of his knees and my brother onto his other knee. My father talked for what I remember as a long time. He spoke to me rather than my brother, and when my brother became restless my father let him down from his knee and went on speaking only to me. Of all that my father said I remember only his telling me that the young woman in the illustration was wearing not a brassiere but an evening dress, and that a young woman would sometimes wear an evening dress because she wanted people to admire some precious piece of jewellery hanging from her neck.

When my father told me this he picked up the page of the newspaper and tapped at a place on the bare chest of the young woman, a little distance above the top of her evening dress. He tapped with his knuckle in the way that he might have tapped at a door that stood closed in front of him.

This morning when I remembered my father's tapping with his knuckle at the bare chest of the young woman, I thought of the top part of the evening dress as being the body of pale blue labelled STREAM SYSTEM. I then saw in my mind my father tapping with his knuckle at the face of his father and also tapping at the yellow-brown grass where the dead rats had once lain before my father had ordered the patients to collect them in kerosene tins and to dump them in the swampy ground that was denoted, many years afterwards, by the words STREAM SYSTEM.

After I had looked at the building that was once the first house that I remember having lived in, I walked back to the slope of grass that had once been the place where the dead rats had lain but was now, according to my map, the bare chest of a young woman wearing an evening dress, the place where my father had tapped with his knuckle, the place where the young woman might have displayed a precious jewel, the face of my father's father.

While I stood in all those places, I understood that I was standing in still another place.

*

As a child I could never be contented in a place unless I knew the names of the places surrounding that place. As a child living in the house of red bricks, I knew that the place to one side of me was Preston, where I sometimes sat with my mother and my brother in the Circle cinema. I had been told by my father that another of the places surrounding me was Coburg, which was the place where I had been born and where I had first lived although I had never remembered it afterwards.

Whenever I stood at the front gate of the house of red bricks and looked around me, I seemed to be surrounded by grasslands. I understood that I was surrounded finally by places, but grasslands, so I saw, lay between me and the places. No matter what place I heard of as being in this or that direction away from me, that place was on the far side of a grassland.

If I looked in the direction of Coburg I looked across the grassland that lay, during the 1940s, on the western side of Plenty Road. Where the suburb of Kingsbury is today, an empty grassland once reached for as far as I could see to the west from Plenty Road.

If I looked in the direction of Preston I saw the grassland sloping past the cemetery and towards the Darebin Creek.

If I looked in the opposite direction from the direction of Preston, I saw only the farm buildings where my father worked each day with the patients, but I had travelled once with my father past the farm buildings and the hospital buildings to a place where the land rose, and from there I had seen more grasslands and on the far side of the grasslands dark-blue mountains. I had asked my father what places were among those mountains and he had said the one word *Kinglake*.

After I had heard the word *Kinglake* I was able to stand at my front gate and to see in my mind the places on the far sides of three of the grasslands around me. I was able to see in my mind the main street of Preston and the darkness inside the Circle cinema. When I looked in the direction of Coburg I saw the dark-blue wall of the gaol and the yellow-brown water of Coburg Lake in the park beside the gaol. My father had once walked with me between the dark-blue wall and the yellow-brown lake and had told me that he had worked as a warder for ten years on the far side of the dark-blue wall.

When I looked in the direction of Kinglake I saw a lake among the mountains. The mountains around the lake were dark blue and the water in the lake was bright blue like the glass in a church window. At the bottom of the lake, surrounded by the bright-blue water, a man sat on a gold throne. The man wore a gold crown and pieces of gold jewellery on his chest and his wrists and gold signet rings on his fingers.

I have mentioned just now three directions that I looked in while I stood at the front gate of the first house that I remember having lived in. I have mentioned the direction in front of me, which was the direction of the place where I had been born, and I have mentioned the directions to either side of me. I have not mentioned the direction behind me.

Behind me while I stood at the front gate of the first house that I remember having lived in was the place where I described myself as standing on the first of these pages. Behind me was the place where I stood this morning looking at a body of yellow-brown water that had been denoted by a body of pale blue in my map, according to what I have written on these pages. Behind me was the place that was the slope of grass where the dead rats once lay; the place that was also the bare chest of a young woman who might have worn an evening dress so that she could display some precious jewel; the place that was also part of the face of a man with a drooping moustache; the place that was also a place just in front of the lips of a young woman who was about to be kissed. Behind me was still another place apart from those places. Behind me was the place that I came from this morning when I set out for the place where I am now. Behind me was the place where I have lived for the past twenty years – where I have lived since the year when I wrote my first book of fiction.

One day while I lived in the house of red bricks, I asked my father what place was in the direction that I have been calling just now the direction behind me. When I asked my father that question he and I were standing near the slope of grass that seemed to us then only a slope of grass that drained the water and other things from the pigsty into the swampy ground. Neither my father nor I would have seen in either of our minds bodies of yellow-brown or of pale blue.

My father told me that the place in the direction that I had asked about was a place called Macleod.

When my father had told me this, I looked in the direction that I had asked about, which was the direction ahead of me at that moment but which was the direction behind me when I looked in the direction of the place where I had been born, and which was also the direction behind me when I stood as I described myself standing on the first of these pages. When I looked in that direction I saw first grasslands and then pale-blue sky and white clouds. On the far side of the swampy ground the grasslands rose gently until they seemed to stop just short of the sky and the clouds.

When I heard my father say the word *Macleod*, I believed he was naming a place that had taken its name from what I saw in the direction of the place. I saw in my mind no place such as Preston or Coburg or Kinglake on the far side of the grasslands in the direction that was in front of me on that day. I saw in my mind only a man standing on a grassland that had risen towards the sky. The man stood on a yellow-brown grassland that had risen towards the pale-blue sky and had come to an end just short of the sky. The grassland had come to an end but the man wanted to go where the grassland would have gone if it had not come to an end. The man stood on the farthest point of the grassland just beneath the white clouds that were passing in the pale-blue sky. The man uttered a short sound and then a word.

The man uttered first a short sound like a grunt. He made this sound while he sprang upwards from the edge of the grassland. He sprang upwards and gripped the edge of a white cloud and then he dragged himself onto the cloud. His gripping and his dragging himself onto the cloud took only a moment. Then, when the man knew that he was safely on the white cloud that was travelling past the edge of the grassland and away out of sight of the man and the boy on the slope of grass below, the man uttered a word. This word together with the short sound made, so I thought, the name of the place that my father had named. The man uttered the word *cloud*.

During the years when I lived with my parents and my brother in the house of red bricks between Coburg and Macleod and between Preston and Kinglake, I often watched the men that my father called patients. The only patient that I spoke to was the young man known as Boy Webster. My mother told me not to speak to the other men that I saw around the place because they were loonies. But she told me I was free to talk to Boy Webster because he was not a loony; he was only backward.

I spoke sometimes to Boy Webster and he spoke often to me. Boy Webster spoke to my brother also, but my brother did not speak to Boy Webster. My brother spoke to nobody.

My brother spoke to nobody but he often looked into the face of a person and made strange sounds. My mother said that the strange sounds were my brother's way of learning to speak and that she understood the meaning of the sounds. But no one else understood that my brother's strange sounds had a meaning. Two years after my parents and my brother and I had left the house of red bricks my brother began to speak, but his speech sounded strange.

When my brother first went to school I used to hide from him in the schoolground. I did not want my brother to speak to me in his strange speech. I did not want my friends to hear my brother and then to ask me why he spoke strangely. During the rest of my childhood and until I left my parents' house, I tried never to be seen with my brother. If I could not avoid travelling on the same train with my brother I would order him to sit in a different compartment from mine. If I could not avoid walking in the street with my brother I would order him not to look in my direction and not to speak to me.

When my brother first went to school my mother said that he was no different from any other boy, but in later years my mother would admit that my brother was a little backward.

My brother died when he was forty-three years old and I was forty-six. My brother never married. Many people came to my brother's funeral, but none of those people had ever been a friend to my brother. I was certainly never a friend to my brother. On the day before my brother died I understood for the first time that no one had ever been a friend to my brother.

*

During the years when Boy Webster spoke often to me he spoke mostly about firecarts and firemen. Whenever he heard a motor vehicle approaching our house along Plenty Road from the direction of either Preston or Kinglake, Boy Webster would tell me that the motor vehicle would be a firecart. When the vehicle proved to be not a firecart, Boy Webster would tell me that the next vehicle would be a firecart. He would say that a firecart would soon arrive and that the firecart would stop and he would climb into it.

In the year when my brother died, which was forty-one years after my family had left the house of red bricks, a man was painting the inside of my house in Macleod. The man had been born in Diamond Creek and was living in Lower Plenty, which means that he had been moving roughly west from his birthplace towards my birthplace while I had been moving roughly east from my birthplace towards his. The man told me that he had painted during the previous year the insides of buildings in Mont Park Hospital.

I told the man that I had lived forty-one years before near Mont Park Hospital. I told him about the farm that was now a university and about the patients who had worked with my father. I told the man about Boy Webster and his talking mostly about firecarts and firemen.

While I was talking about Boy Webster the man put down his brush and looked at me. He asked me how old Boy Webster had been when I had known him.

I tried to see Boy Webster in my mind. I could not see him but I could hear in my mind his strange voice telling me that a firecart was coming and that he was going to get into the firecart.

I told the painter that Boy Webster might have been

between twenty and thirty years old when I had known him.

Then the painter told me that when he had been painting one of the wards of Mont Park Hospital an old man had followed him around, talking to him. The painter had talked to the old man, who said his name was Webster. He told the painter no other name. He seemed to know himself only as Webster.

Webster had talked about firecarts and firemen. He told the painter that a firecart would soon arrive on the road outside the hospital building. He told the painter about the firecart every few minutes and he told the painter that he, Boy Webster, was going to climb into the firecart when it arrived.

The painter's father had been a tramways inspector until he had retired. The painter's father had since died, but the long green overcoat and the black hat with the glossy peak that the painter's father had worn as a tramways inspector still hung in a shed behind the house where the painter's mother lived.

The painter took the long green coat and the hat with the glossy peak to Mont Park Hospital and presented them to the old man known as Webster. He did not tell Webster that the coat and the hat were any sort of uniform. The painter simply presented the coat and the hat to Webster and Webster put them on at once over the clothes he was wearing. The old man known as Webster then told the painter that he was a fireman.

On the day before my brother died, I visited him in his hospital ward. I was his only visitor during that day.

A doctor in the hospital had told me that he was not prepared to say what particular illness had affected my brother, but the doctor believed that my brother was in danger of dying. After I had seen my brother I too believed this.

My brother was able to sit in the chair beside his bed and to walk a few steps and to sip from a glass, but he would not speak to anyone. His eyes were open, but he would not turn his eyes in the direction of anyone who looked at him or spoke to him.

I sat beside my brother for most of the day. I spoke to him and I looked at his face, but he would not speak to me and he would not look in my direction.

For much of the day I sat with my arm around my brother's shoulders. I believe today that before that day in the hospital I had not put my arm around my brother's shoulders since the evening in the house of red bricks when I had tried to teach my brother what a brassiere was used for.

From time to time while I sat with my brother, a woman in one or another uniform would come into the room. The uniform would be white or yellow-brown or one or another shade of blue. Whenever one of these women would come into the room I would wait for her to notice that I had my arm around the shoulders of the patient. I wanted to tell the woman in a loud voice that the patient was my brother. But none of the women seemed to notice where my arm was resting while I sat beside the patient.

Late on that day I left my brother and returned to my house in Macleod, which is nearly two hundred kilometres north-east from the hospital where my brother was a patient. My brother was alone when I left him.

On the following night I was told by telephone that my brother had died. My brother had been alone when he died.

At the funeral service for my brother, the priest said that my brother was now content because he had now become what he had been waiting for more than forty years to become.

On the Sunday after I had first thought of giving a pendant as a present to the young woman who was about to become my wife, the married sister of my father arrived at the house where I had sat looking at the jewellery catalogue.

One of my unmarried aunts asked my married aunt to show me her pendant. At that moment I looked at the part of my married aunt's body that lay between her throat and the place where the top of her evening dress would have been if she had been wearing an evening dress.

My married aunt was wearing not an evening dress but what I would have called an ordinary dress with buttons at the front. Only the top button of the dress was undone, so that I saw when I looked at my married aunt only a small triangle of yellow-brown skin. I saw no part of a pendant anywhere in the yellow-brown triangle.

When my unmarried aunt had told my married aunt that I had been admiring the pictures of pendants in the jewellery catalogue and that I had never seen a pendant, my married aunt moved one of her hands to the lowest part of the triangle of yellow-brown skin below her throat. She rested her hand in that place, and with the ends of her fingers she unfastened the second-top button at the front of her dress.

From the time when I had first heard that my married aunt was the owner of a pendant, I had supposed that the main part of the pendant was in the shape of a heart. When my aunt undid the second-top button of her dress I expected to see, somewhere on the skin between her throat and the place where the top of her evening dress would have been if she had been wearing an evening dress, a tapering golden heart.

125

When my married aunt had unfastened the second-top button at the front of her dress, she pushed apart with her fingers the two parts of the front of her dress and she found with her fingers two sections of fine golden chain that had been lying out of sight behind the front of her dress. With her fingers my aunt lifted the sections of chain upwards a little and then she scooped into the hollow of her hand the object that had been dangling at the end of the sections of chain. My aunt then lifted her hand out from between the two parts of the front of her dress and turned the hand towards me so that the object at the end of the sections of chain lay in the hollow of her hand where I could see it.

I understand today that the object in the hand of my married aunt was a piece of polished opal whose shape was roughly oval and that the object would have been of several shades of blue and other colours as well. But my aunt showed me for only a few moments what lay in her hand, and while she showed me the object she turned her hand a little so that I saw first what I thought was an object all of pale blue, then what I thought was an object all of dark blue, and then, after my aunt had slipped the object down again behind her dress, only the yellow-brown of part of the skin between my aunt's throat and the place where the top of her evening dress would have been if she had been wearing an evening dress.

Just before I began to walk this morning from Macleod towards the first house that I remember having lived in and the first view of grasslands that I remember having seen, I read something that brought to my mind the first body of blue water that I remember having seen in my mind.

I read in the pages of a newspaper that a famous stallion will soon arrive in this district. The stallion will arrive, according to what I read, from a famous breeding stud in the Vale of Tipperary, which is the part of Ireland where the father of my father's father arrived from when he arrived in this country.

The famous stallion will be used for serving more than fifty mares at the Mornmoot Stud, which is at Whittlesea, on the road between Preston and Kinglake. The name of the famous stallion is Kings Lake.

The only married woman from among my father's five sisters was the wife of a primary teacher. As a married woman she lived in many districts of Victoria. At the time when my aunt showed me her piece of polished opal of roughly oval shape, she and her husband were living about four miles inland from the place where I often sat with my back to the Southern Ocean and looked at the pages of a jewellery catalogue or of the *Saturday Evening Post*. The name of the place where my aunt and her husband lived is Mepunga East. In the same district is a place named Mepunga West. In maps of that district the word *Mepunga* appears only in the names of those two places.

Much of the text of *The Plains* was formerly part of the text of a much larger book. The larger book was the story of a man who had lived as a child in a place named Sedgewick North. If any map had been drawn of the district around that place, the map would have shown a place named Sedgewick East a few miles south-east of Sedgewick North. The word *Sedgewick* would have appeared only in the names of those two places.

The man who had lived as a child in the place named Sedgewick North had believed as a child that his district lacked what he called a true centre. Sometimes he used instead of the words *true centre* the word *heart*.

For some of the time while I was writing about the district around Sedgewick North, I saw in my mind some of the places around Mepunga East.

For most of his life my brother was said to be backward, but he was able to do some things that I have never been able to do.

Many times during his life my brother was able to travel in an aeroplane, which is something that I have never been able to do. My brother was able to travel in aeroplanes of different sizes. The smallest aeroplane that my brother travelled in contained only my brother and the pilot. My brother paid the pilot to take him through the air above part of the southern boundary of the mainland of Australia. While my brother was in the air he recorded by means of a camera and a roll of colour-film some of what he saw around him. I did not know that my brother had been in that air until after he had died. After my brother had died, the prints from that roll of colour-film were given to me.

Whenever I look nowadays at those prints I wonder whether my brother had become confused while he was in the air above the southern boundary of the grasslands of Australia, or whether the pilot of the aeroplane had tried to amuse or to frighten my brother by causing the aeroplane to travel sideways or even upside down through the air, or whether my brother had simply pointed his camera at what any man would see if he stood at the place in the air where the grasslands of Australia obviously have a mind to go.

When I look at those prints I seem sometimes to be looking at a place all of pale blue and sometimes to be looking at a place all of dark blue and sometimes to be looking at a place all of yellow-brown. But sometimes I seem to be looking from an impossible vantage-point at dark-blue water and, on the far side of the dark-blue water, the endless yellow-brown grasslands and the endless pale-blue sky of America.

(*AGE MONTHLY REVIEW* 8, NO. 9,
DECEMBER 1988–JANUARY 1989)

SECRET WRITING

Thirty years ago, in 1962, I was in my early twenties and living alone in a rented flat in the Olivers Hill district of Frankston. I was living in Frankston because I was a teacher at Overport Primary School in Towerhill Road. I was teaching at Overport because I had previously applied for my position there. I had applied for my position there and for fifty and more positions in other schools in other suburbs of Melbourne, because I had no wish to teach in any one-teacher school in any country district of Victoria. I had no wish to teach in any one-teacher school because I wanted my evenings and weekends for myself.

In 1962 I taught a class of forty-eight fourth-grade children. They were well-mannered children, and I looked forward to being with them each day. (The only day when I was reluctant to set out for school was the day when President Kennedy of the United States of America warned Mr Khrushchev of the Union of Soviet Socialist Republics to turn back his ships from Cuba or be blown up along with half the human race.) I owned no car at that time, and I used to walk from my flat to school before eight each morning. Many of those mornings must have been cold and rainy, but as I write these words I remember only fine mornings when I looked at the birds in the gardens that I passed in Kars Street or Jasper Terrace or when I looked up through trees towards The Crest and The Spur and The Ridge and wondered how anyone could earn enough money to be able to live in the houses I glimpsed there.

I looked forward not only to meeting my class each day but also to being at the school itself. Overport School is on a hill overlooking Frankston, and the room where I taught in 1962 had a view of a wide segment of Port Phillip Bay. From my desk I could see as far as Ricketts Point in the north and far out past the shipping lanes in the west. At one side of the playground was a last patch of what might have been the original scrub of the Mornington Peninsula, where a few echidnas still lived.

On a certain warm morning in 1962 I had taken my class out into the playground for a period of what was described on the timetable as phys. ed. The children were divided into four teams, and every child wore either a red or a blue or a green or a gold sash. My class was as fond as I was of competitive games and the statistics they gave rise to: tables of premiership points, votes for best players, record times . . . On the certain morning, the four teams were playing tunnel ball. We were far away from the school building, and the children were free to yell as they pleased. At a certain moment during the game of tunnel ball on that certain morning, the yelling of the children and the closeness of their competition and the warmth of the sunshine and the distant view of the blue bay and of the purplish haze over the inner suburbs made me feel as though I had found already, young as I was, the life I was going to lead for the next forty years.

At the moment just mentioned, and for a few moments afterwards, I thought of myself as someone who would be a teacher in primary schools for the rest of his working life. The schools where I would teach would all be in suburbs of

Melbourne, and not drab inner suburbs but older suburbs with trees in their streets or outer suburbs with views of mountains in the distance. On warm spring mornings I would dream in the sunshine while my class romped or competed. On rainy afternoons I would be dry indoors while my class worked quietly at their desks. At the end of each year, and twice during each year, I would take a longish holiday. I would never enrol in any courses to improve my qualifications or my career prospects. I would never aspire to be a head teacher. I would remain until the end of my working life a humble classroom teacher in the last room along the corridor or the farthest room around the corner in a wing of the main building, watching the seasons change and the years pass outside my windows.

I have not yet mentioned the chief item in the vision that came to me on that certain morning in 1962.

I had decided early in 1962 that I was going to spend most of my evenings and my Sundays during the rest of my life writing prose fiction. If a young man made that decision in 1992, he might well have read dozens of books of fiction by contemporary Australian writers. A young would-be writer of 1992 might well have heard dozens of Australian writers of fiction reading from their works. The young would-be writer might have met some of those writers and spoken to them at writers' festivals. The young would-be writer would certainly have read many published accounts of interviews with Australian writers. The young man who decided while he was living in Frankston in 1962 that he was going to write fiction for the rest of his life could have named no more than four or five living Australian writers – not because he was ignorant of Australian writing but because very few books of Australian fiction were published in the early 1960s. The young man at Frankston had never heard a writer read in public and had never attended a writers' festival because no writer read in public in those days and no writers' festivals were held.

If I were a young writer starting out in 1992, I would sometimes be tempted to despair when I thought of how many other writers are already being published. In 1962, what tempted me sometimes to despair was the thought of how *few* Australians seemed to be writing fiction or getting it published. I felt in 1962 that writing fiction was almost an un-Australian thing to be doing. And even if, so I thought, Hal Porter and John Morrison and George Turner were scratching or tapping somewhere far away, surely no one else but myself was trying to write fiction in Frankston or in any of the suburbs I could see around the curve of the Bay. In 1962 I thought of the writing of fiction as more European or even more American than Australian. I could more easily imagine someone doing what I was doing in a suburb of Leeds or Wichita than in a suburb of Melbourne.

When I started to write fiction I was a secret writer, and I expected to be a secret writer even after my first book had been published. I expected that I would never earn an adequate income from my writing (how right I was!) and that I would have to go on working as a teacher until my retirement. The Education Department of Victoria had in those days a regulation forbidding teachers from undertaking other forms of regular paid employment. I did not know in 1962 whether the writing of fiction – even unpublished fiction – would be regarded as breaking this regulation, but I had no wish to make my case a test case. If ever I were published, it would be under a pseudonym.

I had other reasons for wanting to be a secret writer. I had met many fine men and women among my fellow primary teachers but hardly any I would have cared to discuss my secret writing with. (I believe today that the difficulty lay as much with me as with my colleagues. I have never enjoyed talking about my writing to any but a handful of people.)

I did my secret writing in 1962, and for three years afterwards, on most Sundays and on three or four evenings each week. During those years I told five or six persons about my secret writing. I confessed my secret only after I had drunk too much alcohol and usually to young men who were in the same state as I myself, so that no harm resulted. However, one of the persons who learned my secret was a young woman whose affection I was hoping to earn. This was in 1964, the third year of my career as a secret writer. The young woman was not greatly impressed to hear about my secret writing, and she was dismayed to learn that I had never considered studying for a university degree although I was well qualified to do so.

I got my degree by studying part-time for five years. During one of those years I became married to the young woman who had not been impressed by my secret writing. During each of those years I added a few pages to my secret writing in the summer holidays. Then, only a few days after my last university exam, I was offered a job that would take me away from the classroom, and I accepted.

The new job was in the Publications Branch of the Education Department, which produced technical publications and lighter reading for teachers and students. Now, my job required me to write and edit by day, and I worked alongside other writers, even if they were not writers of fiction. Yet I went on with my secret writing by night and on Sundays, and on a certain evening in 1970, nearly nine years after I had begun to write fiction in secret, I finished the final draft of a book-length piece of fiction that I believed would be publishable.

Then I did what is surely the most secretive thing a secret writer can do: instead of trying to get my hundreds of pages of fiction published, I hid them away and told no one about them. Why I did this I never understood, but it was my last secretive act as a secret writer. After a year had passed, I showed my writing to another secret writer. He had heard from some non-secret writer that a certain publisher was interested in publishing Australian fiction, and he urged me to stop being a secret writer and to take my writing to the certain publisher. This was in 1973, more than ten years after I had begun my career as a secret writer.

I took my writing to the publisher who told me my writing would be published if I would shorten it by half. I took my writing home and shortened it by a third. The publisher published my writing as a book with my true name on the cover. I was no longer a secret writer.

I have not been a secret writer for nearly twenty years, but I would like to go back to being a secret writer again. I think I enjoyed secret writing better than my later sort of writing. As a secret writer, I was more free to write what pleased me. During the years of my secret writing, nobody ever asked me to look at their own writing and to comment on it. During those years, no editor of a magazine ever approached me at a party and asked me to write a piece for her magazine.

I would like my next book to be published with a pseudonym on the cover. Better still, I would like the book to be published with no author's name on it. But I would like more than that. I would like all books of fiction to be published without their authors' names. I would like all writers to be secret writers. Then, readers would read books with more discernment. I believe many readers are too much influenced by the names on the fronts of books.

A few years ago, at a seminar for a group of editors, I handed around photocopies of a typed page of prose fiction. I asked the editors to correct any error of punctuation or of sentence structure that they might find on the page. The editors found many errors – as I had expected they would. After the editors had corrected the many errors on the page, they were surprised to learn from me where I had found the page. I told the editors that I had changed the names of the persons and the places mentioned on the page but that the page was otherwise just as it appeared in a recent prize-winning novel by one of Australia's best-known writers of fiction.

(*TIRRA LIRRA*, VOL. 3, NO. 1, SPRING 1992)

THE BREATHING AUTHOR

I cannot conceive of myself reading a text and being unmindful that the object before my eyes is a product of human effort.

Much of my engagement with a text consists of me speculating about the methods used by the writer in the putting together of the text, or about the feeling and beliefs that drove the writer to write the text, or even about the life story of the writer.

What I am about to tell you today is the sort of detail that I would have been eager to know if it had been my fate to be a person who was drawn to read these books (points to the stack of his books nearby) rather than the person who was drawn to write them.

I have for long believed that a person reveals at least as much when he reports what he cannot do or has never done as when he reports what he has done or wants to do.

I have never been in an aeroplane.

I have been as far north from my birthplace as Murwillumbah in New South Wales and as far south as Kettering in Tasmania; as far east as Bemm River in Victoria and as far west as Streaky Bay in South Australia. The distance between Murwillumbah in the north and Kettering in the south is about 1,500 km. It so happens that the distance between Streaky Bay in the west and Orbost in the east is about the same. Until I calculated these distances a few days ago, I was quite unaware that my travels had been confined to an area comprising almost a square, but my learning this was no surprise to me.

I become confused, or even distressed, whenever I find myself among streets or roads that are not arranged in a rectangular grid or *are* so arranged but not so that the streets or roads run approximately north-south and east-west. Whenever I find myself in such a place, I feel compelled to withdraw from social intercourse and all activities other than what I call finding my bearings. These I try to find by reference to the sun or to roads or streets the alignments of which are known to me. I know I have found my bearings when I can visualise myself and my surroundings as details of a map that includes the northern suburbs of Melbourne and such prominent east-west or north-south thoroughfares of those suburbs as Bell Street or Sydney Road.

My trying to find my bearings takes much mental effort, and I fail more often than I succeed. I often believe I have succeeded but later refer to maps and find that my visualised map was wrong. When I discover this, I feel compelled to attempt a complicated exercise that I have probably never succeeded at. I am compelled first to recall the scene where I tried to find my bearings, then to recall the visualised map that proved to be wrong, and last to try to correct my remembered self, as it were: to relive the earlier experience but with the difference that I get my correct bearings. I sometimes feel this compulsion many years after the original event. While writing these notes, for example, I was compelled to recall the evening in November 1956 when I visited for the first time the suburb of Brighton, on Port Phillip Bay. It was my last day of secondary school, and my class had to meet at the home of the school captain and later to take a train into Melbourne to see a film. I arrived in Brighton by bus, in the company of boys who knew their way around that quarter of Melbourne. Later, when our class arrived on foot at Brighton Beach railway station, I stood with them on the platform where they had gathered, but I was convinced that we were waiting for the train *from* Melbourne. After the train had arrived and we had boarded, I remained convinced for some time that we were travelling *away from* Melbourne, and my peace of mind was continually disturbed during the rest of the evening by my wondering how I had so utterly lost my bearings at the railway station. Just now, as I said, I was compelled to relive that experience of more than forty years ago, but I failed yet again to understand how the map of Melbourne in my mind had been stood on its head.

I cannot understand the workings of the International Date Line.

I cannot understand how the values of the currencies of different nations can change in relation to one another – much less how anyone can profit from this phenomenon. I can talk glibly as though I *do* understand these and many other such matters, but in truth I do not.

I have no sense of smell and only a rudimentary sense of taste. When I hear or read of a thing as possessing a smell or an aroma, I feel no sense of deprivation but imagine at once a barely visible emanation from the thing: a mist or a cloud of droplets, always distinctively coloured: delicate colours for aromas said to be faint or subtle, and rich colours for strong smells.

I tend to think of words as written things rather than spoken things. While I speak, I often visualise my words as being written somewhere at the same time.

I am often able to remember the appearance on the page of a passage that has interested me. If I try to learn by heart any poetry or prose, I do so by visualising the printed page and reading it in my mind. When, in 1995, I began to learn the Hungarian language, I used both textbooks and cassettes and I conversed with native speakers. Even so, I always see written in the air, as it were, the words of my conversations nowadays in Hungarian; and whenever I recite from memory the Hungarian poems that I know, I always see the poems printed on the pages that I learned them from.

I have been told that when I mention some person or thing out of sight I often point in the direction in which I suppose the person or thing to be while I speak. I seem to do this just as readily for persons or things on the other side of the world as for persons or things in an adjoining room. I have often been observed pointing towards the presumed dwelling place or site of some person or event from the past.

I have never owned a television set.

I have watched few films during my lifetime and hardly any in recent years. Throughout my life, I have had much trouble in following the story-lines of films and making the necessary connections between the rapidly changing images. I have watched no more than a half-dozen live theatrical performances during my lifetime and none during the past twenty-five years. I recall little of what I watched. I have never watched an opera.

On almost every occasion when I have watched a film or a theatrical performance, I have been made to feel embarrassed and uncomfortable by the exaggerated facial expressions, the excessive gestures, and the frank speech of the characters, and I have been relieved afterwards to resume my life among persons who seem to use facial expressions and gestures and speech as much as I use them: in order to conceal true thoughts and feelings.

I cannot recall having gone voluntarily into any art gallery or museum or building said to be of historic interest.

I have never worn sunglasses.

I have never learned to swim. I have never voluntarily immersed myself in any sea or stream. I have sometimes stared at running water in small rivers or in creeks inland, but I have never felt any urge to contemplate any part of any sea. I was told only five years ago by my mother that I was taken to the seaside for the first time at the age of six months, that I began to scream as soon as I saw and heard the sea, and that I went on screaming until I was taken out of sight and hearing of it.

I have been described by my wife and by several friends as the most organised person they have ever known, and I admit to a love of order and of devising systems for storing and retrieving things. My library is meticulously ordered, as are the many filing cabinets full of my letters and journals and manuscripts and typescripts and private papers. I have some-times thought of the whole enterprise of my fiction-writing as an effort to bring to light an underlying order – a vast pattern of connected images – beneath everything that I am able to call to mind.

And yet I seem to have a fear of the systems devised by other people, or if not a fear, then an unwillingness to engage with those systems or to try to understand them. I have never touched any button or switch or working part of any computer or fax machine or mobile telephone. I have never learned how to operate any sort of camera. (I am able, however, to operate several kinds of photocopier, and I do so often.) In 1979 I taught myself to type using the index finger of my right hand alone. Since then, I have composed all my fiction and other writing using the finger just mentioned and one or another of my three manual typewriters.

I have a rough understanding of the Dewey Decimal System, but I have never learned how to use a library catalogue. Until about 1980, I sometimes went into one or another library and looked along the shelves labelled, so I recall, from 800 to 899 and sometimes took from those shelves one or another book and looked into it. In about the year 1980, electronic devices began to be common in libraries. As from about the year 1980, I have sometimes gone into one or another library to attend a book launch or a similar function but never to look for any book or other item or to try to use any catalogue or similar aid or to approach any employee for advice. The years when I have followed this policy include thirteen years when I was a lecturer in one or another institute of tertiary education and three years when I was a senior lecturer in a university.

I studied English One, English Two, and English Three in successive years as part of my course for the degree of Bachelor of Arts in the University of Melbourne. (I followed this course from 1965 to the end of 1968 when I was aged from twenty-six to twenty-nine years.) I came close to failing several of my examinations and essays during my three years as an English student, but in several other examinations and essays in English I earned high marks. All through those years, I had the utmost difficulty in understanding what exactly I was supposed to *do* as a student of English and what exactly I was supposed to report of my doings in my examinations and essays. At the same time, I suspected that the teaching staff in the Department of English had equal difficulty in understanding what *they* were supposed to be doing when they lectured or conducted tutorials or marked essays or examination papers.

I have read hurriedly Terry Eagleton's book *Literary Theory: An Introduction*, Blackwell 1983. I have read much less hurriedly Wayne C. Booth's book *The Rhetoric of Fiction*, University of Chicago Press. (I have read both the 1961 edition and the revised 1983 edition.) I do not recall having read any other book on literary theory or related subjects.

I was pleased to find in Wayne C. Booth's book a persuasive theoretical account or several matters that I had felt convinced of for many years but had been unable to articulate. I am thinking in particular of the extraordinary chart in the Afterword to the second edition. (I have always liked charts and diagrams and graphs; I have sometimes tried to use such means to clarify for myself matters rarely quantified or charted.) Booth's chart has two long columns. In one column are listed the variety of authors and in the other column the variety of readers that may be said to exist while a work of fiction is being written or read. Most of the authors exist in the minds of readers, and most of the readers in the minds of authors. The first of the variety of authors in the chart is called by Booth the Flesh-and-Blood Author or, elsewhere, the Breathing Author. This worthy is described as 'immeasurably complex and largely unknown, even to those who are most intimate'.

I hardly need to add that Booth compiled his chart from a consideration only of the acts of reading and writing. His chart would have been vastly more complicated if he had tried to take account of our situation today: of a breathing author's meeting in person with some of his varieties of reader. (The chart includes a so-called career-reader, which term might apply to some of you. Check Booth for yourselves.)

I tried to use charts and diagrams to help me plan most of my book-length pieces of fiction, but as I went on writing I was always obliged to abandon the planned format. I was uneasy whenever I first found that I could not make my fiction conform to the shape that I had planned for it, and sometimes afraid that what I was writing might be aimless or shapeless. Long before I finished each book, however, I was reassured that it was a unified whole. I even believed that I might have been able to represent the finished book by a complicated chart or diagram, although I never tried to do so. I still sometimes think of one or another of my pieces of fiction – whether book-length or short – as being not page after page of text but a many-coloured array of interconnected images. Some of these images are as simple as the green stone surrounded by the bluish haze in 'Emerald Blue', while others are as complex as the race for the Gold Cup in *Tamarisk Row*. When I think of my fiction in this way, I am somewhat of a mind with the narrator of 'In Far Fields', who saw his fiction as resembling a map of a country district in which the small towns were images and the roads connecting the towns were feelings. I am also not unlike the young man in the early pages of *The Plains* who won over the great landowners by using coloured pencils and graph paper to illustrate the history of culture on the plains.

I acknowledge that my liking for charts and diagrams may be a primitive, even a childish habit of thought. In my understanding of history, or time past, for example, I rely on the simple diagram that I found nearly fifty years ago in a secondary-school history textbook: the time line. I cannot think of the history of this planet in any other way than as having taken place on a seemingly endless series of oblong cross sections of earth and sea, each a hundred years long, so to speak. Each oblong ends abruptly at the end of the century that it denotes. The following oblong begins far away to the left (as I see it) of this point, the oblongs or centuries being parallel to one another in the darkness of no-space and no-time. If I think of the life of Marcel Proust, for example, I have no trouble in seeing the writer and all his surroundings come to an end on the last day of 1900 and then reappear far away at the very beginning of the twentieth century. The narrator of my story 'First Love' might have seen exactly thus.

During the sixteen years from 1980 to the end of 1995, I was a full-time teacher of fiction-writing. I taught always in the same tertiary institution, but the place had three different names and three different modes of administration during those sixteen years. In its third guise, the place was known as Deakin University and the mode of administration was such that I retired early, at the age of fifty-five, thereby reducing my income by five-sixths, rather than endure another year in the place.

For as long as I was a teacher of fiction-writing, I looked out for and collected statements made by writers and others on the vast subject of how fiction might be written or understood. I did not collect only statements that I myself could agree with. I collected a range of statements so that I could usually offer my students not only my own views on fiction-writing but also an opposing view. While preparing this text, I decided not to look through my collection of writerly statements but to cite the two or three that are still often in my mind more than five years after I last stood in front of a class. I have chosen two.

I offer the first statement without any comment. I found about twenty years ago in a book review in the *New York Times* the statement by the poet Robert Bly that the writer should learn to trust his obsessions.

I found perhaps even longer ago in the Introduction to *Great Short Works of Herman Melville*, published by Harper and Row in their Perennial Classics Series in 1969, the following statement by a man otherwise unknown to me, Warner Berthoff. 'A story well told, so that it has the power to enter permanently into the imagination . . . always tells us two things. It says "here is what happened" and it will say further "this is what it is like to have knowledge of such happenings . . . and to undertake the task of opening such knowledge to others".' I found this statement when I had already written much of the fiction of mine that has been published. I do not say that the statement by Warner Berthoff, whoever he is or was, taught me anything I had not previously known. However, that statement had been for me ever since I found it my preferred means of explaining why much of my fiction is as it is; why the narrator of much of my fiction looms, as it were, larger than any character in the fiction. Berthoff's statement also happens to explain in a few words many of the arguments of Wayne C. Booth.

I can put this point another way. For most of my time as a writer of fiction, I have wanted not to have my reader take my writing as an account of a world whose existence the reader and I might agree on. I can put this point still another way. The aim of most of my fiction is not that the reader should sympathise with any character or share the feelings of any character, much less believe in the reality of any character. No, the aim of most of my fiction is that the reader should believe in the reality of the narrator of the fiction.

I often told my students that a writer of my sort of fiction is a technical writer. The task of this sort of writer is to report in the plainest language the images that most claim his attention from among the images in his mind and then to arrange his sentences and paragraphs (and, if applicable, his chapters) so as to suggest the connections between those images. This may seem to a gathering of scholars a niggardly account of how I came to write books of fiction that provide you with such a field of enquiry. For me to say that I wrote what I wrote simply by describing some of the contents of my mind – is this too easy a way out for me?

Perhaps I should do for you people here today what I often did for my classes in Introductory Fiction Writing. I used to tell each of those classes, in about my fifth session with them and a few weeks before their first fiction assignment was due, that a person paid to teach others a skill ought to be able to exercise that skill in front of the others and to give a full and clear account of the exercising. Then I used to do in front of the class something that few teachers of fiction-writing can have done in a classroom. Sometimes by writing key words on the whiteboard, and sometimes by miming with my hand in the air the writing of sentences that I spoke at the same time aloud, I tried to show my students how I would have begun an as-yet-unwritten piece of short fiction.

I used to crib just a bit in my demonstrations of fiction-writing, but I explained to my students that I was cribbing and why. Most of my pieces of short fiction have begun with a single image: sometimes a simple image, sometimes a detailed image. The image would have appeared to me many a time before I understood that it would later be the source of a piece of fiction. The image would have bothered me, perhaps, or pleaded with me, or simply stared at me for days or even months before I noted its details and filed my note in my file for such notes. My cribbing in front of my classes consisted in my beginning my demonstration with an image the details of which had previously been filed in the file just mentioned. I could never have begun to write a piece of fiction at my own desk, let alone in the sometimes uneasy atmosphere of a writing class, unless I was working with an image that I could trust.

If I were to try in front of you people today to write in the air the beginnings of a piece of short fiction, I would begin by reporting in a sentence or two certain details from the image that I recalled this morning when I was trying to recall images the details of which I have noted during recent years in the file mentioned earlier. I would report details that might seem banal or trivial to you people, although I would assure you of my confidence that those details were full of meaning for me. Why else, I would ask you rhetorically, would the image and all its details have stayed in my mind for year after year when so many other images had disappeared? In short, I would write in the air between you and myself one or two sentences reporting that a hen crouched on the ground in an unkempt front garden of a house of red bricks on a certain afternoon of the fifth decade of the twentieth century when the sky was filled with close-packed and fast-moving grey and black clouds and when the same wind that drove the clouds across the sky ruffled tufts of feathers on the crouching hen.

I would report much more of this single image. I would report that a male child who happened to notice the hen from the rear seat of a motor car while it drove out of the unkempt garden and who wondered why the hen was crouching when it might have been foraging noticed in an instant before the car turned out of the garden and northwards towards a place called Kinglake, where he had never yet been and about which he had often speculated, that the wind had ruffled in the same instant not only the hackles of the hen, which were of a rich, copper-orange colour, but a few of the under-feathers, which were of a glossy black colour, and that the ruffling of the under-feathers had caused to be exposed to the wind the head of a chicken, only a few days old and of a pale, creamy colour.

I would then pause in my reporting and would assure you that I was not, most emphatically not, writing a sort of autobiography while I was reporting the details of the hen and the ruffled feathers, even though I myself happened to have lived in a house of red bricks during a few years of the decade mentioned earlier and even though my father happened to have won so much money on Dark Felt in the Melbourne Cup of 1943 that he bought a huge brown Nash sedan and took his wife and children for Sunday drives for several months until he had to sell the Nash sedan to settle his latest debts with his bookmakers. If I were writing a sort of autobiography, I would say to you good people, I would be reporting the sort of detail just mentioned. I would be reporting my memories of the summer of 1943–44, when my father took me and my two brothers and my mother for a drive every Sunday. I would be reporting conversations, shaping anecdotes, trying to suggest motives . . .

I would go on with my reporting of details of images. I would report that the noise of the car caused the hen to rise to its feet, enabling the male child in the back seat to notice that the cream-coloured chicken was the *only* chicken of the black hen with the copper-orange hackles and causing the child to wonder why his father, who owned the hen and the chicken and many other hens and chickens and roosters, had not dashed the head of the chicken against a post as he had dashed the heads of a number of other chickens in the past when he had not wanted to have the mothers of the chickens looking after only one or two or even of a handful of chickens when she might have rejoined the flock of hens that laid eggs daily.

I would report a few details of a few more images. In the meanwhile I would remind you that my noting the details of image after image was not at all what is sometimes called *free association*. I would point out that my looking at the details of the image of the hen with the ruffled feathers brought to my mind a succession of images that I took no interest in: images of, for example, the garden where the hen sat in the wind or of the house nearby. I would explain that I usually discovered each of the images that I needed for a piece of fiction while I stared in my mind at the details of a previously discovered image and looked out for the detail that winked at me. Soon after I had noticed the winking of the detail of the copper-orange hackles of the hen, for example, I had seen in my mind for the first time, so I believed, an image of an illustration in a book for children in which illustration a number of infant children were either dead or asleep or beneath the surface of a stream the water of which had been coloured an orange-gold colour by the artist.

I would have been aware, as soon as I had used the word *winking* in my report of my means of discovering images, that one at least of you, my listeners, would have wanted me to explain further what exactly I saw when an image winked at me. And I would have been prepared to explain, when one of you questioned me after I had finished talking to you, that a detail of an image does not wink in quite the way a human being winks to another. The detail of an image, being almost always something other than a human face, has no eye with which to wink, and must signal to me by a sort of flickering or fluttering or nodding or trembling. Even so, I choose deliberately the word *winking* to describe this primitive signal to me from some patch of colour or some shape in my mind. I so choose, because my seeing the signal never fails to make me feel reassured and encouraged as many a person must feel after being winked at by another person. And I choose the word winking in this context because a wink from one person to another often signals that the two persons share a secret knowledge, so to speak, and I often feel, after some detail in my own mind has winked at me, that I have been shown proof that the farthest parts of my own mind are friendly towards me; that whatever may be hidden in those far parts of my mind is willing to reveal itself to me; that all is well in what passes with me for the world.

If I had tried to write in the air in front of you the beginnings of a piece of fiction, I might have gone on to report that the detail of the water in the stream where the children were asleep or dead would have caused me to see in my mind, and to prepare to write about, an image of a man lying just below the surface of a greenish wave as it broke about twenty metres from a beach in the southwest of Victoria a few years after the day when the wind ruffled the feathers of the hen with the one chicken. The man just mentioned was neither dead nor asleep but demonstrating to his children, who were standing in shallow water near the beach, that the human body is of its nature buoyant and that water need not be feared. And at about this point in my demonstration of my beginning a piece of fiction, I would have understood (and would have told you at once of my so understanding) that the title of the piece of fiction would probably be 'King-in-the-Lake'. And if I had thought that the matter was not evident to you, I would have ended my demonstration by telling you that I have always considered titles important and have looked for the title of each of my pieces of fiction among the words relating to the most important of the images that gave rise to the piece.

I read a little, many years ago, of the writings of C.G. Jung and Sigmund Freud but soon lost interest. I found the notion of an unconscious mind required of me the same sort of belief that I had formerly, as a church-going young person, been expected to place in angels and demons and the like. And no theoretical account of the personality has ever seemed to me as convincing as the demonstrations offered in fiction of even average quality of the infinite variability of human-kind. In this, as in so many other matters, I have preferred to ponder particular instances rather than to consider general assumptions.

I should add here that I have never been able to under-stand, much less believe in, any theory of the evolution of species. Such notions as that primitive organisms are capable of promoting their own interests, let alone the interests of their descendants – such notions seem to me even more far-fetched than anything in the Book of Genesis.

*

I have never felt much interest in systems of mythology and have found tedious at best those works of literature the meaning of which derives from some personage or story or theme or motif in Greek or any other mythology. However, at some time around my fortieth year I began to understand that some of my own writing derived some of its meaning from details in a body of beliefs that might be called my own *mythology* or *cosmology*. If asked to defend this rather pompous-sounding claim, I might have to quote from or refer to some of my writings that are still unpublished and will remain so during my lifetime.

I believe I may be unable to think abstract thoughts. I studied Philosophy One at the University of Melbourne in 1966, when I was aged twenty-seven, but after I had handed in my first written exercise I was taken aside by my tutor and told that I did not seem to understand what philosophy itself was.

I have come to believe since that my tutor was right. Even so, I managed to obtain second-class honours in Philosophy One by being able to recall during examinations particular paragraphs from textbooks and particular comments from lecturers and tutors; to write summaries of what I remembered; and to write also a few comments that I imagined a person such as myself might have written during a philosophy examination if that person had understood what philosophy itself was.

Later in my university course, I enrolled under a misapprehension in a certain unit and found myself studying in translation the works of the renowned Arab philosophers of the Middle Ages. I passed this unit by the same means that I had used to pass Philosophy One, but with the important difference that I discovered in the works of a philosopher whose name I have long since forgotten a statement that I not only seemed to understand but from which I drew a sort of inspiration as a writer of fiction. The statement was to the effect that everything exists in a state of potentiality; that is to say, anything can be said to have a possible existence.

I am not unaware that my cherished fragment of philosophy may well have come originally from Greek philosophy or may be a commonplace of that philosophy. Many things that I cherish have found their way to me by winding, circuitous routes.

A thing exists for me if I can see it in my mind, and a thing has meaning for me if I can see it in my mind as being connected to some other thing or things in my mind.

In my view, the place we commonly call the real world is surrounded by vast and possibly infinite landscape which is invisible to these eyes (points to eyes) but which I am able to apprehend by other means. The more I tell you about this landscape, the more inclined you might be to call it my mind. I myself often call it my mind for the sake of convenience. For me, however, it is not just *my* mind but the *only* mind.

Apart from what lies right now within the narrow range of these two eyes (points again to eyes), everything that I am aware of or have ever been aware of is somewhere in the far-reaching landscape of (my) mind. Of course, I acknowledge the existence of other minds, but such is my view of things that I can only see those minds and their contents as being located where all other imagined or remembered or desired entities are located – in the landscape of landscapes; in the place of places; in my mind.

One piece of fiction always gives me a special satisfaction whenever I look back on it: 'A Quieter Place than Clun' in

Landscape With Landscape. The narrator of that piece struggles for many years to have some of his writing published and, at the same time, to conceive of some coloured image or diagram that will fill a gap or void that he imagines within himself. He achieves only limited success in each enterprise. At the age of thirty-four, he has a story published in a small magazine; and he is somewhat content, as years pass, to think of road maps of Victoria or diagrams of Melbourne streets as emblems of his essential self. At the end of the piece of fiction, the character finds himself again confused; large areas of his mental landscape have been called into question; but if I know him, he will be able at last to correct his image of himself, perhaps in somewhat the way that a family might have introduced quarterings into its coat-of-arms during the course of its history.

My feeling of satisfaction when I look at 'A Quieter Place' is wholly selfish. It may seem to you an unworthy sort of satisfaction; a perverted sort of satisfaction. I confess that I feel satisfied with my having achieved what the isolated and rather ineffectual character of my fiction had not achieved: I have achieved it by having had published the body of fiction of which 'A Quieter Place' is a part *and* by being sometimes able to see all that fiction as defining me in the way that the narrator of 'A Quieter Place' wanted to see himself defined. Yes, I sometimes have the experience of seeing my fiction as an emblem of myself or an heraldic device representing myself or even as a large part of myself. And I derive much satisfaction from so seeing.

But what exactly do I see? I have sat just now for several minutes trying to answer that question. Sometimes while I sat, I seemed to be trying to see an image of every image in my writing – a fantastic chandelier of images: a gigantic three-dimensional mandala, or a ten-thousand-sided hologram of coloured scenery. But I could not hold this sort of image in my mind long enough to admire it. In the end, there occurred to me an emblematic scene, by which I mean a scene that might have been reported nowhere in my fiction but a scene that stands for the essence of that fiction.

A man sits in a book-lined room in a house of many rooms. The window-blinds in the room are drawn, but the light at their edges tells me that the day outside is hot and bright. The silence in the room tells me that the house is surrounded by a wide and grassy and mostly level landscape. In the book-lined room, the sitting man sometimes reads and sometimes writes. What he mostly reads about or writes about is, perhaps, a woman or, perhaps, another wide and grassy and mostly level landscape further off from his own.

I have sometimes asked myself the idle and fatuous questions what should I have done differently? or, what would I do differently, given a second chance? Of all the idle and fatuous answers that have occurred to me, the only answer that might interest you people is my declaring sometimes that I should have written all my fiction with no regard for the conventional terms *novel* or *short story* or *novella* but should have allowed each piece of my fiction to find its way to its natural end.

I started out wanting to be a poet. I thought as a boy that the purpose of writing was to move people; to cause persons to feel more deeply. For most of my youth, the writing that moved me was poetry. I was often moved deeply by poetry. Among the first works of prose fiction that moved me deeply were *Wuthering Heights*, by Emily Brontë, and *Tess of the D'Urbervilles* by Thomas Hardy, and it is by no means a coincidence that I first read these books, and several other books by Thomas Hardy, during the year when I began to think of writing prose fiction.

I had another reason for wanting to be a poet. I believed for long that a writer of prose fiction had to have a deep understanding of other people and – more alarming still for me – had to be able to *imagine* or *create* believable characters. As someone who had been isolated during childhood and adolescence, who was preoccupied with his own moods and daydreams, and who was consistently baffled by the behaviour of other people, I thought I was qualified only to be a poet.

However, I found poetry extremely hard to write for as long as I tried to write in rhymed, or even unrhymed, metrical lines. I found it somewhat easier to write what I believed was free verse, but I thought it was cheating to call such writing poetry. I began to write prose believing that I could express more freely in prose than in poetry what I wanted to express. However, I believed for several years that my prose would have more meaning if I allowed myself not to observe the conventions of English grammar. At about the time when I was writing the first drafts of the first pages of *Tamarisk Row*, I came to understand that I could never conceive of a network of meaning too complex to be expressed in a series of grammatical sentences. All of my published prose consists of grammatical sentences, although the second-last section of *Tamarisk Row* consists of four grammatical sentences interwoven. One of my greatest pleasures as a writer of prose fiction has been to discover continually the endlessly varying shapes that a sentence may take. I tried to teach my students to love the sentence. I sometimes suppose that the existence of the sentence bears witness to our need to make connections between things. I still sometimes think of trying again what I tried and failed to do as a young writer: to write a work of fiction consisting of one single grammatical sentence containing at least several thousand words.

I have not read widely during my lifetime. You might be shocked if I were to name for you some of the so-called great works of literature that I have never read. I have tended to read several times those books that appealed to me rather than to read widely.

At my age, I need not ask myself which books I would take to a desert island. All I need do is to ask myself which books I would like to read yet again during the years left to me. I list them in alphabetical order according to authors' names: the various collections of short fiction by Jorge Luis Borges; *Wuthering Heights*, by Emily Brontë; several collections of short fiction by Italo Calvino, together with *The Castle of Crossed Destinies* by the same author; *Independent People* and *World Light*, by Halldor Laxness; *Remembrance of Things Past*, by Marcel Proust.

I offer two supplementary lists. The first is for Australian literature: *The Fortunes of Richard Mahony*, by Henry Handel Richardson; the Langton novels, by Martin Boyd.

The second supplementary list is for Hungarian literature; *Puszták Népe* and *Konok Kikelet*, both by Gyula Illyés.

I encourage you to think of each of my seven published books as a report of some or another part of the contents of what I call my mind. And yet it seems to me, at the age of sixty-two, that the half-million words and more of my published books together reveal not a great deal about the interests and concerns of the person I believe myself to be.

About ten years ago, while I was trying to write what would have become a huge book of fiction with the title *O, Dem Golden Slippers*, I found myself unwilling to go on with my writing. I have still not fully understood what it was that stopped me from going on with that book and caused me to write little fiction for the next few years. I will try, however, to explain what I can explain.

My drawing back from *O, Dem Golden Slippers* had something to do with my being a husband and a father of adult children. If I had been, as Marcel Proust was, neither a husband nor a father, or if I had been, as D.H. Lawrence was, a husband but not a father, I might not have drawn back. For thirty years past, I had written fiction without caring how many readers might be so careless or so foolish as to suppose that the narrator or the chief character of any piece of my fiction closely resembled the breathing author; but in 1991, in the fifty-third year of my life, I drew back. I drew back partly because what I was about to write might have seemed to certain readers to have revealed more than was seemly for a man of my years, a husband and a father, to have revealed. But I drew back for another reason: quite a different reason. In writing certain passages of *O, Dem Golden Slippers*, I had discovered certain images and certain connections between images such as seemed to reveal to me that my thirty years of writing fiction had been nothing less than a search for just that sort of discovery. I have tried to describe this discovery to several persons by writing that I seemed to have crossed, at last, the country of fiction and to have discovered on its farther side a country no less inviting. I will be hardly less evasive today, but will assert something that should provoke you to think about the purpose of fiction.

I always took seriously the writing of fiction. I told my students that no one should write fiction unless he or she absolutely *had* to write it; unless he or she could not contemplate a life *without* the writing of fiction. During all the years while I wrote fiction, I assumed that I would always write fiction, but I believe now that I was driven to write fiction only so that I could make the discovery mentioned in the previous paragraph. My first thoughts after I had made the discovery were to the effect that I had somehow failed as a writer of fiction; that I had stopped short of writing the sort of fiction that might have enlarged my reputation enormously or made of my collected works a magnificent edifice. My later thoughts were to the effect that what had happened ought to have been expected. I had undertaken the writing of my books of fiction exactly as another sort of person may have undertaken a serious study of some difficult matter. My writing was not an attempt to produce something called 'literature' but an attempt to discover meaning. Why should I feel surprise or disappointment if the result of my writing seven books of fiction was my discovery of something of much meaning to myself and my deciding that the writing of fiction was no longer of much importance to me?

I have been somewhat evasive as to details in the previous paragraphs. However, I have written detailed reports for scholars of the future, if there be any such. I have stored these reports in what I like to call my archives. In those archives are copies of all my letters of the past thirty years; a journal that I kept on and off from 1958 until about 1980; numerous drafts of all my published works of fiction and of several unpublished works; notes for many works of fiction that I have not yet tried to write; and many notes from myself to an imagined scholar of the future, explaining candidly some or another matter of possible interest.

All of my archives, which at present fill about nineteen drawers of steel filing cabinets, will become the property of my sons after my death and will, I hope, end up in a library

in, I hope, Australia. For several years now, I have been annotating my papers so as to make clear any passages that might
not be clear to a reader of the future. When my annotating is
completed, my collected papers will comprise a remarkably
detailed documentation of my life and my thinking. However,
so candid is this documentation that my papers will not be
available to the curious or the scholarly reader until several
persons apart from myself have died.

I have been an eager reader of writers' biographies for
many years and have noted often the problems faced by
biographers when letters or other papers are lost or scattered
or censored by one less than honest. I believe my collection
of papers will one day supply anyone interested with a body
of material as bulky, as detailed, and as candid as any that
I have read about.

It occurred to me this afternoon, Sunday 8 July 2001, that
I have not changed much during the last fifty years. I was at
my desk when this thought occurred to me. I was not obliged
to be at my desk. I had actually found myself with a free hour,
something that seldom happens with me. But I had chosen,
almost unthinkingly, to go to my desk and to find something
that I could do with pen and paper: annotating some page
from my archives, perhaps, or translating a stanza from my
collection of Hungarian poetry, or checking the records that
I keep of the two hundred racehorses that I bet on.

Before I began any of these tasks, I sat back and turned
my attention loose, so to speak.

My desk is a small student's desk. It stands in a corner of
my room, facing a blank wall. (I prefer to leave a wall blank
rather than to decorate it in any way.) Just to my left are thick
curtains concealing a window. (I prefer to keep the curtains

and blinds closed whenever I am indoors.) Just to my right is the nearest of the six grey or white filing cabinets that stand around my room. While I was looking at one or another of the blank walls or the grey or white filing cabinets, I thought of myself nearly fifty years ago, in the early 1950s.

If I had found myself with a free hour of a Sunday afternoon in those days, I would have chosen to spend it alone, with a pen and paper handy. I seem always to have hoped to learn more by waiting behind drawn blinds, by daydreaming, by jotting things down on paper than by going about the world or even by reading.

Because today is Sunday, I soon thought of one large difference between myself in the 1950s and myself today.

It would be hard to overemphasise the influence on me of my upbringing as a Roman Catholic in the 1940s and 1950s. I was one month short of my twentieth birthday when I chose not to believe any longer, but before then I had been an unquestioning and sometimes a devout Catholic. This means that from the earliest days that I can recall until my young adulthood, I saw the visible world as being surrounded by an invisible world consisting of four distinct zones, namely heaven, hell, purgatory and limbo, and peopled by countless angels, demons, souls of dead human beings, and a God consisting of three subjoined divine persons. More than this, I lived during all those years never doubting that a goodly number of the invisible beings just mentioned were watching my every movement and aware of my every thought. Some of the beings were very much concerned for my welfare, by which I understood that they wanted me to join them in their eternal happiness after I had died. Others of the beings were reproachful on account of my seldom remembering to pray for their souls; these were my dead relatives and forebears. Still others of the beings were malevolent towards me and would have felt a perverse satisfaction if they could have ensured that I would spend eternity in hell with them after I had died. These, of course, were the devils who arranged, among their many other machinations, that I should often find in newspapers or magazines pictures of young women in tight bathing costumes or low-cut evening dresses.

More than forty years ago I ceased to be a believing Catholic, but I have never been able to think of the visible world, the so-called real world, the place where I sit writing these notes – I have never been able to think that this is the *only* world. I might go further and say that the notion of this being the only world seems to me hardly less preposterous than the notions imparted to me as a child by my Catholic parents and teachers and ministers of religion. I might go further still and report that I feel confident that a part of me will survive the death of my body and will find itself after that event in a world presently invisible to these eyes (points yet again to eyes). I might go even further yet and say that I have lighted on what I consider sound evidence for these beliefs of mine. But to go further would probably embarrass all of us. It seems to me that a writer of fiction might disturb a group of scholars less by confessing to some unsavoury sexual proclivity than by announcing his belief in an afterlife and claiming to have seen evidence for his belief.

Anyone reading through my archives after my death will find detailed notes on the matters alluded to somewhat coyly just now, but no one should expect to receive after my death any message from the Other Side. One life as a writer will have been enough.

*

Someone has written that all art aspires to the condition of music. My experience is that all art, including all music, aspires to the condition of horse-racing.

Only two forms of art have ever affected me deeply: literature and music. Whenever a passage of literature or of music has affected me deeply, I have been compelled to pause in my reading or in my listening and to try to observe the details of the last hundred metres or so of one or another race contested by one or another field of horses that has suddenly appeared on the home straight of one or another racecourse in my mind.

I have sometimes glimpsed details of the many-coloured jackets of the riders of the horses, and there has sometimes come into my mind the name of one or another of the horses, but more than these few items I have never learned. I have thought more than a few times during the past few years that a task at least as worthy as the writing of a further work or works of fiction would be for me to try to draw the outlines of some of the racecourses just mentioned or the details of the many-coloured jackets; to try to list the names of the horses and of their trainers, jockeys, owners; to record details of the races as Clement Killeaton was reported to have recorded details of races in *Tamarisk Row*, my first published work of fiction, or as the nameless Tasmanian was reported to have done in 'The Interior of Gaaldine', which is the last piece in the last book of mine to have been published as of now.

(EDITED VERSION OF A PAPER GIVEN TO THE GERALD MURNANE RESEARCH SEMINAR, UNIVERSITY OF NEWCASTLE, 20–21 SEPTEMBER 2001; PUBLISHED IN *I HAVE NEVER WORN SUNGLASSES*, HEAT 3, NEW SERIES, 2002)

THE ANGEL'S SON: WHY I LEARNED
HUNGARIAN LATE IN LIFE

Nem a való hát: annak égi mássa
Lesz, amitől függ az ének varázsa . . .

The song itself is not what matters most; it has a heavenly other
from which the magic descends.

JANOS ARANY (1817–82)

Many persons are fluent in more than one language, but my setting out some years ago at the age of fifty-six to teach myself Hungarian provokes comments and questions from those who get to hear of it.

Like much else seen in hindsight, my enterprise seems to me now to have been inevitable. In my early years I envied various persons for various reasons, but my strongest envy was always directed at those who could read and write and speak and sing in more than one language.

The first such persons that I was aware of were the Catholic priests who celebrated the mass and other services in the churches that I attended in the 1940s. As a child, I considered the Latin spoken by the priest to be the verbal equivalent of the vestments that he wore. I have always been much taken by rich fabrics and by colours, emblems, and motifs. Long before I understood a word of Latin, I responded to the sounds of its syllables as to so many arrangements of white lambs or red blood-drops or gold sunbursts on silk chasubles of the so-called liturgical colours. I had the usual child's image of the deity as an old man of stern appearance, and I could never imagine either of us as feeling warmly towards, let alone *loving*, the other, but I was moved by the ceremonies that I supposed he himself had prescribed for his worshippers, and I was not at all surprised that he had to be addressed on solemn occasions in a language known only to his priests.

I was only seven when I resolved to learn the sonorous Latin language. I found in my father's missal pages with parallel Latin and English texts. I imagined I could learn the language simply by finding which word in the Latin text was the equivalent of one or another word in the English text and so accumulating a Latin vocabulary to be drawn on as required. I was brought up short when I found that the Latin for *God* might be *Deum*, *Deus*, *Dei*, or *Deo*. This and other problems made Latin seem to me perverse and arbitrary by comparison with my native English but only increased my desire eventually to master Latin. In the meanwhile, I derived unexpected pleasures from hearing or, more often, mishearing the language.

During the last half-hour of the school day on the first Friday of each month in the mid-1940s, the pupils of St Kilian's School and of the Marist Brothers' College, after having walked in separate formations for a short distance along McCrae Street, Bendigo, from their respective classrooms to the parish church of St Kilian's, there formed almost the whole of the congregation during the ceremony of the Benediction of the Most Blessed Sacrament, or Benediction for short. The pupils of the College were all boys. The pupils of the School were mostly girls, although the three most junior classes had equal numbers of boys and girls. Most of the College sat on one side of the central aisle. Most of the School sat on the other side. I was one of the junior boys of St Kilian's, whose view of the sanctuary was mostly blocked by the heads and shoulders of the older girls.

One of the hymns sung during Benediction was known by its first word, *Adoremus* (Let us adore . . .). On the afternoons that I am writing about, I knew none of this. The words of the ceremony would have been printed somewhere in the back of my father's missal, but I had never read them. I understood much later that the words of *Adoremus* were intended to sound as praise for the Eucharist, but to me as a child in Bendigo nearly sixty years ago they brought quite other meanings.

No one in the seats around me could have tried to sing any of the hymns, but from the seats towards the front of the church came a slow, drawn-out version of the sacred words. Evidently, the nuns and the brothers had taught the words to their older pupils, but the singers, self-conscious and unsure, produced what sounded to me mainly of sadness and struggle.

On some afternoon that I will never recall, I first heard the four syllables of the word *Adoremus* as the English phrase *sons of the angels*. Afterwards, on many an afternoon that I well recall, I heard that phrase not only while the singers droned out the Latin *Aaa . . . dor . . . e-e . . . mus*, but whenever else the vague sounds of the Latin allowed me. Years later, when I had learned by heart both the English and the Latin words, I still preferred to dwell on my own mental imagery while I sang under my breath my private words.

Sons of the angels . . . On the afternoon mentioned in the previous paragraph, I had already seen numerous pictures of angels. I had been assured by teachers and by priests that I enjoyed the exclusive attention of my own angel: my guardian angel, as she was called.

I did not hesitate before using the pronoun *she* in the previous sentence, but I had to struggle somewhat as a child before
I could feel sure of the gender of my invisible guardian and
companion. I had wanted from the first a female angel, but
the same people who assured me of the existence of angels
insisted that they were neither male nor female. In fact, the
appearance of angels in devotional pictures tended towards
the masculine, and the only angels with names – the archan-
gels Gabriel, Raphael, and Michael – were always spoken of as
males. Still, the beardless faces, the long hair, and the flowing
robes of pictured angels did not much hinder my imaginings.
In time, my female guardian began to appear to me, although
never as an image of a whole female form. (I have long since
come to accept that when I do what is usually denoted by
the verb *to imagine*, I am able to call to mind only details and
never wholes.) Her shining hair and flawless complexion
I would have derived mostly from advertisements in the
Australian Women's Weekly. Her voice would have come from
one or another radio play or serial. I could hardly have been
knowledgeable enough to imagine a character or personality
to go with her angelic appearance, but if I know anything of
the person I was fifty and more years ago, I can be sure that
her distinguishing quality was trustworthiness. I could have
confided anything to her.

What I have written just now about my angel is not at all
meant to report that she and I were already on familiar terms
during my childhood. According to my teachers, my angel had
been appointed as my guardian at the moment of my birth.
I was not reassured, however, by the words of the prayer that
we recited in class every day: 'O Angel of God, my guardian
dear . . . / ever this day be at my side . . . ' I have heard long
since that theologians can justify our having to ask in prayer

for benefits that would have come to us by right, but in my childhood my having to plead daily with my angel to stay with me prevented me from feeling that she was permanently mine. In any case, even my child's sense of the rightness of things would have told me that the precious boon of angelic companionship ought to have been earned; to have come at some cost. (And while I wrote the previous sentence I recalled having heard in class from one or another pious nun that our every sin caused our guardian angels to turn away from us.)

Sons of the angels . . . Whatever bond I might sometimes have felt between myself and my angel, when I sang under my breath to the melody of the hymn from the Benediction service all angels, my own included, seemed far away. The sons of the phrase were not at all related filially to the angels. In my mind, an angel was a virginal female impossible to associate even with spiritual motherhood, let alone bodily. The word *son* in Bendigo in the 1940s was commonly heard in streets and schoolyards. Among schoolboys it served as *mate* or *pal* or *cobber* would have served at other places and times. It was heard even more often as the form of address used by men towards boys other than their sons. The sons of the angels were to me the juniors, the nondescript rag-tag mob of boys milling around far beneath the gaze of the heavenly beings who were their guardians but who still kept their distance. And whether or not each angel had as yet been appointed the guardian of each son, I sensed that the angels in general were disappointed with us sons in general. We played childish games or fought each other in the dusty schoolyard, scarcely aware that we were entitled to live a different life indeed, if only we could have been mindful of angelic ways.

Sometimes, if I struggled to imagine the angels and their ways, I attributed to angels some of what I seemed to have discerned in the older girls of St Kilian's School, who would have been thirteen or fourteen years of age. These persons moved gracefully and spoke in quiet voices; they had a love of cleanliness and order; and, so I had learned one morning when I was sent on an errand by my teacher to the eighth-grade classroom, they could recite the Latin and Greek roots of many English words. Thoughts of the older girls often led me to think of their counterparts across the aisle of the church: the older boys of the Brothers' College.

From a very early age, I had been interested in what I thought of as *romance*. I learned what I could of the subject from the same source that had taught me the word itself: the women's magazines that were the chief reading matter in our house. At the time when I daydreamed about the angels and their sons, I assumed that older boys and girls were even more interested than I was in romance. I was seldom without a girlfriend. My chosen female was sometimes a girl from my own class, who was almost always left unaware of my having chosen her. She was sometimes a girl from a higher class who might not even have known of my existence. And she was occasionally an adult: a woman whose face I had seen in a drawing or a photograph in one of the magazines mentioned already. I needed a girlfriend chiefly so that I could see one or another detail of a female image in my mind or could sense a female presence there. But I had also a vague notion that our relationship, such as it was, was a foreshadowing of the future. At some vague time in some remote place, my wife-of-the-future and I might walk together on the street or sit together in our motor car whereas now we met only at the sides of my mind.

Sons of the angels . . . I had met with no boy of my own age who was interested in romance, but I could not believe that the man-sized senior boys of the Brothers' College had not each chosen for himself a girlfriend after having inspected during many a religious ceremony the rows of older girls across the aisle. And so I was able sometimes to hear the drawn-out Latin as one or another message from the boy-men to their chosen females. We may seem ungainly and roughly spoken, so the message might have run, but we admire your gentleness and your demureness and we wait in hope for some glance or some sign of encouragement from you. We are only the sons as of now, but we are willing to learn the ways of the angels.

It should be apparent that my various imaginings during the Latin hymn were anything but orderly or consistent. I might have been thinking at one or another time of the yearning of the older boys for the girls across the aisle and yet thinking a moment afterwards of angels and mortals. Whatever might have been the details of my thoughts, the recurrent theme was of the enforced separation of personages who deserved to be united.

I heard from the radio one evening in Bendigo part of the story of two such personages. My parents used to seem uneasy whenever I became interested in radio plays or serials meant for adults, and they were apt to switch off the radio if the characters talked too much about romantic matters or if they sighed or murmured or otherwise suggested that hugging or kissing may have been going on. If I was eager to listen to something from the radio, I used to make a show of being involved in some game in a corner of the room. Sometimes I even disguised my interest by leaving the room for short periods. I cannot recall that my parents censored the radio adaptation of Henry Longfellow's narrative poem 'Evangeline' on the evening when I heard it, but I took away from it only a jumble of impressions – perhaps because

I knew hardly anything about the history or geography of North America. What I remembered afterwards were the cries of the separated lovers during their lifelong search for one another, each calling the other's name in a landscape that I imagined as a vast prairie. And I would not have failed to notice, and to add to my stock of secret meanings, that the name of the young woman, *Evangeline*, had at its core the word *angel* and that the young man, Gabriel, was named after an angel.

It might have fitted more neatly with the themes of this piece of writing if I could have reported that the various separated personages often in my mind were separated not only by their differing natures or qualities and by their distance from each other in space but also by their speaking each a different language. What I seem mostly to have imagined was that the angelic/female personage was at home not only in the English spoken by the sons, myself included, but also in a language spoken only among her own superior kind. The higher language I thought of mostly as Latin, but I was sometimes able to imagine fragments of other such languages. In my confused response to the radio version of 'Evangeline', for example, I heard the occasional French proper nouns as suggesting that the heroine spoke her own private language in addition to the English of the narrative. At such times I was keenly aware that I knew only English, and yet I seemed to myself at other times to have acquired fragments of a language from elsewhere.

During my childhood, songs or stories faintly heard or vaguely understood would at first annoy and frustrate me but would later encourage me to compose a private music and a private mythology so rich in meaning that I dwell on them nowadays at least as often as I hear in my mind the music of acknowledged masters or as I recall my having read one or another work of literature. According to my best recollections, the first hit parade, as it was called, was broadcast from 3BO Bendigo in 1948. The so-called number-one song when I first listened in was 'Cruising Down the River', sung by Arthur Godfrey. The last line of the chorus of the song was 'Cruising down the river on a Sunday afternoon'.

In the 1940s, so I recall, crooners such as Bing Crosby caused a certain sort of young woman to shriek as her later counterpart would shriek on hearing rock-and-roll stars. But hit parades and crooners had made few inroads into the staple content of music programmes when I was listening to the wireless-set in the mid-1940s. Whole programmes were given over to bel-canto, arias from operettas or even operas, popular songs from earlier decades (the name Al Bowley comes to mind), and especially dance music (Victor Sylvester). I mention these details lest the reader suppose that when I went far down into the backyard on many a Sunday afternoon in the years mentioned already (in a provincial city where the silence was broken as often by the clip-clop of cart-horses as by the noises of motor-cars) and listened deliberately to the faint rhythms and the snatches of melodies from one or another neighbouring house, I heard the brutal thumping or the animal-wailing that would be their equivalent today. The sounds that I heard were teasingly varied.

At the time, I was not concerned as to where they came from: the sounds that I thought of as Sunday-afternoon music or far-away music. I suspect now that most of them came not from neighbouring houses but from a bungalow in the backyard of one of the houses. It would much better suit my purposes in this piece of writing if such had been so. A backyard bungalow stood behind many a house in the 1940s. The bungalow was hardly more than a shed, often unlined, and its occupant was usually a widower or a bachelor, often a heavy drinker, who took his meals with the family in the house. In later years, I learned that the bungalow was a necessary adjunct to many a lower-middle-class house in the south-eastern suburbs of Melbourne, where I attended secondary school. In a typical house with two bedrooms, the daughters occupied the second bedroom while the sons had for *their* bedroom a backyard bungalow. How often the widowers and bachelors of Bendigo in the 1940s masturbated in their bungalows I have no way of knowing, but I have spoken with several men of my own generation who were thankful that they occupied backyard bungalows during their adolescence and early manhood and could masturbate in comparative privacy.

My mood on most Sunday afternoons was somewhat melancholic. Sometimes the hints of music that I heard only deepened my mood; at other times they relieved it. Sometimes the hints seemed only to remind me of how far I was from *my* land of heart's content, wherever and whatever it might have been. The inhabitants of *that* land were close to the source of the music, and their feelings were on that account far richer and more sustaining than my own mere longings. But at other times I believed myself capable of composing from the faint thumpings and the fragments of phrases something fit to be chanted or sung in places far from my dusty backyard. My melancholy was more often deepened than relieved; the dwellers in the far landscape seemed on most Sundays utterly unaware of me; and yet I was sometimes able to imagine myself drawing nearer them. Sometimes I saw them looking towards me as I approached them along one of their splendid avenues or across one of their vast lawns. They made, at first, no move to welcome me, but then they understood that I was calling to them in their own language or singing one of their own songs.

I am able to recall a number of fragments from the many that I used to chant or sing in what I hoped might have been the language of Elfland or Paradise or Idaho, and I am about to cite one such on this page. I called to mind readily just now the sounds and the melody – I have often heard them in my mind during the fifty and more years since I first heard them – but when I came to *write* them just now, I found that the non-English syllables had no written equivalents in my mind. I had to choose between several possible written versions of those syllables because for most of my life I had merely heard them; I had never seen them as writing in my mind.

> La boola boola, la boola boola
> Sealie off-oof,
> Kar sealie off-oof,
> And let the rest of the world go by.

The last of these lines came from a popular song of the mid-twentieth century, and I sang the line exactly as I had heard it in the song. I sang the first three lines to a melody that I had devised myself, probably by varying one or another tune that I heard often from the radio. As for the syllables of those lines, most may have come from my having misheard the words of songs – not only English words but German or Italian also. What interests me much more than the origins of this fragment, however, is the fact that I devised it, sang it often, and got from my singing a certain mood or a state of feeling – all this without once translating the text, so to speak. During most of my life, these lines have had considerable meaning for me, even though most of the words have never had specific meanings. In short I invented, to the best of my child's ability, a foreign language so that I could feel more intensely or see further than I was enabled to feel and see by the sounds of my native language.

I think of myself nowadays as a person who *reads* words rather than *hears* them. At school or at university, whenever I wanted to memorise a passage I studied it in such a way that I was able afterwards to visualise its appearance on the page. I often notice myself reading in the air, as it were, my own and other persons' words during a conversation. For some years during my childhood, I felt obliged to write with my finger on the nearest surface every word that came to my mind. Walking to school, for example, I scribbled continually with the point of my index finger on the smooth leather of my schoolbag, trying to record in writing the onrush of my thoughts. For how long, I wonder, has English been for me only a written language?

The first sentence that I recall having composed in writing is 'The bull is full'. I wrote this sentence with pencil on paper in either February or March in 1944 and showed it soon afterwards to Eleanor Warde, the part-owner with her husband of the house where my family lived at that time in rented rooms. Mrs Warde was a handsome woman with dark hair and was, according to my best recollection, the first female person that I was drawn to confide in. I can hardly have written my sentence in order to report something I had observed or had had reported to me. The sentence is almost certainly the result of my taking pleasure from the sounds of English before I became accustomed to words as writing.

During my lifetime I have become competent, to varying extents, in six languages, but I have only once learned a language by hearing its sounds. That language was, of course,

my native English, which was for me no more than a spoken
language during the few years before I began to read and write.
(I am able to recall a few occasions when I heard for the first
time one or another English word and when I subsequently
spoke it often to myself in order to savour some peculiar
state of feeling that the word gave rise to. I recall even such
details as the place where I was standing and the fact that
I was strangely affected by the word in question, but of the
feelings aroused by the word I recall only the faintest hint.
I can see in my mind, for example, a white window-curtain
being lifted by the wind while I repeat aloud the word *serenade*. I am no more than three years old, and I have recently
heard that word for the first time; I heard it pronounced in a
deep voice by a male announcer during a radio programme.
The sound of the word has a strange effect on me as I say it
aloud, but I recall nothing of that effect today. When I look
at the word *serenade*, even in the context of this paragraph,
I am hardly aware of it as having any sound; it appears to me
as a written word around which float a few images.)

Evidently, the one language that I first learned as a system
of sounds became for me long ago a system of written words
and sentences. I became so used to English as a medium and
so much occupied with the subject matter of my reading or
writing that I seldom noticed or was affected by the audible
qualities of my first language.

During my twelfth year, I was fluent in the Latin of the mass.
I was an altar boy in the suburb of Melbourne where my family
then lived. I had been given at first a booklet with the altar
boys' responses printed in it, but I soon learned its contents by
heart and thereafter recited either with eyes reverently closed
or while staring at the pattern of dark-green fleurs-de-lis on

the pale-green sanctuary carpet or at the embroidered imagery and lettering on the priest's chasuble or the altar-cloth. I had learned the Latin at first by reading it, but the sounds of the prayers had been more or less familiar to me since my early years. And although I knew well the English equivalent of each Latin sentence, I had not much understanding of the syntax of the Latin. In short, I was more likely to hear myself reciting the Latin than to see it unrolling as a text in my mind, and I was easily able to cut myself adrift from the meaning. Admittedly, there were days when I tried to be devout and to utter the Latin responses as prayers, but I was much more inclined to use my small store of foreign syllables for my own purposes.

I began to enjoy hearing myself recite, aloud but to myself alone, the longest piece of Latin from my store. This was the confessional prayer, the *Confiteor*. When I recited it under the fig-tree in my favourite corner of the backyard in 1950, it seemed inordinately long, but when I recited it just now at a leisurely pace, it took no more than thirty seconds. I have forgotten what thoughts were in my mind during my earliest recitations under the fig-tree, but a time came when I began to hear the chanted Latin as someone might have heard faintly from a distant radio the description of a horse-race.

I have written elsewhere about the importance to me of horse-racing, but there may be some reader of this writing who needs to be told that I have got from horse-racing during my lifetime more meaning than I have got from literature or music or any other branch of what is generally called culture. For whatever reasons, images of horse-racing appear in my mind whenever I have begun to feel intensely about any matter. The most common but by no means the only images are of the last hundred metres of various races. A few of these are races that I have watched in the past. Others are races between horses I cannot even name on racecourses whose very whereabouts are a mystery to me. I am not aware of having any influence on the progress or the results of these races-in-the-mind; I watch them only as a spectator. Even so, I understand as soon as the field of horses comes into my view that I ought to follow the progress of one particular horse, and this I do, having recognised the horse by some imperceptible sign or by a sort of instinct. This horse is only sometimes the eventual winner; at other times it fails by a narrow margin or as a result of misfortune.

My hearing the *Confiteor* as a description of a horse-race was a new advance for me. Before then, I could expect to see genuine, unbidden horse-racing images only as a result of hearing certain passages of music or of reading the last page of one or another piece of fiction. I did not become wholly unaware of the meanings of the words: the phrase *Beatae Mariae semper Virgini*, for example, always brought to my mind a set of racing silks in the Virgin's colours of blue and white. However, I tried to hear the Latin as I heard it formerly in St Kilian's, Bendigo: as sounds full of a meaning that I myself was free to discover.

The *Confiteor*, being a comparatively brief prayer, gave rise mostly to racing imagery appropriate for the finishes of sprint races. The longest of the prayers recited aloud during the old Latin mass was the Nicene Creed. This was recited by the priest alone; as an altar boy I was not required to learn a word of it. Impelled, however, by my love of long-distance races for staying horses, I determined to learn the Latin of the Creed and, in time, I did so.

These paragraphs hereabouts report events and processes that occupied years of my childhood and adolescence. While the *Confiteor* was still the only sequence of foreign sounds that gave rise to racing imagery, it became closely associated with a particular race, the winner of that race, and the trainer of that winner.

The racing game, as it was often called in the 1950s, was vastly different from the racing industry, as it is called today. Fifty years ago, the successful and admired trainers were those who said least to journalists and even avoided being photographed. They defied the public to learn about the prospects of their horses and claimed to know nothing of the plunges that were launched on them by well-informed stable commissioners. My father pointed out to me at race meetings the trainers he most admired and told me what he knew of their ways. The man I came to admire most died long ago, never suspecting that his name would one day appear in a literary magazine or, more likely, never suspecting that such magazines existed. Of the many achievements of A.R. (Alf) Sands, the one that became most firmly lodged in my mythology was his trying for nearly two years to bring to peak fitness a horse with such frail legs that a moderately fast track-gallop could send it lame. Alf Sands finally prepared the horse for a sprint race at Moonee Valley. Since the horse had not raced for so long, stable followers secured lucrative odds. The horse led clearly all through the race, carrying the stable colours of gold with red stars. The name of the horse was Lone Saint.

The Nicene Creed is not only longer but also much richer in content than the repetitious *Confiteor*. While chanting the creed, I was sometimes pleased to have the meaning of one or another bold Latin declaration as the mental background for my images of horse-racing. In time, two Latin passages became, as it were, part of this background.

Et exspecto resurrectionem mortuorum . . . This is the second-last utterance of the creed, and the English equivalent in my missal was 'And I look for the resurrection of the dead'. After I had begun to study Latin at secondary school, I came to feel that the English in my missal ignored the import of what seemed to me the most striking detail of the Latin: the prefix ex- in the word *exspecto*. Whenever I chanted the sentence, I got from the single syllable of that prefix a sense of the speaker as not merely *looking for* but *looking out for* and even *straining to see* and finally, leaving behind the literal meaning, *hoping to see*. Then, on whatever forgotten day in the 1950s this last sense lodged in my mind, there must have appeared soon afterwards the sequence of visual imagery that has been ever since bound up with it. A man stands at the rear of a crowded grandstand overlooking a racecourse. The man's head is turned towards a field of racehorses just then entering the straight of the racecourse. The head of every other person in the crowd is likewise turned, but the head of the man is the central detail in my vision – although I am able almost simultaneously to see in my mind the field of racehorses that he sees with his eyes and even the one horse that he looks out for and strains and hopes to see. The face of the man is often the face of Alf Sands, although the character and the life-story of the man belong not to Alf Sands, whom I know only by sight, but to an elemental figure from my mythology, a figure whose fate is inseparable from the successes and failures of racehorses.

In order to give to this piece of writing a coherent shape, I have simplified some matters. On the many occasions when I have chanted the Nicene Creed, I have been able to experience much more than is reported in the previous paragraph. Mental events, as any self-aware person knows, are hardly affected by what are called *time* and *space* in this, the visible world. While I chanted the second-last utterance of the Nicene Creed, dwelling on the sound of the word *exspecto* and seeing in my mind the face of the man who was hoping to see his horse prominently placed and even being aware of the axial lines of the man's character, the field of horses in the race in my mind was still approaching the turn into the straight. After the word *mortuorum* in the printed version of the creed in my missal was a full point. After the word *mortuorum* in my chant, I paused for less than a second. During that interval of time, I was able to comprehend an event that might have taken twenty and more seconds if it had happened in the world from which my mental images were derived. In short, by the time when I began to chant the first syllable of the last utterance of the creed, the field of horses in my mind had passed along the straight of the racecourse in my mind and had arrived at the winning-post.

My chanting of each section of the creed was meant to have the sound appropriate to the equivalent section of the imagined race. But the sense that I got from the words of the last two utterances was such that I was never required to imitate the agitated, almost-falsetto voice of the race-commentator describing the progress of the field along the straight and towards the winning-post. I heard that sound in my mind during the pause of less than a second mentioned above, just as I saw in my mind during that pause images arising from the progress of the field towards the post, but when I chanted the first syllable of the last utterance, my voice had become noticeably more quiet. Out of a turbulence of possibilities had come something not to be doubted; the race had been decided.

Et vitam venturi saeculi. Amen. This is the last utterance of the Nicene Creed. (I consider the *Amen* as inseparable from the phrase preceding it.) The English version in my missal was 'And the life of the world to come. Amen'. As I write this today, I am annoyed by the shoddy punctuation in my missal. What I have called the last utterance has been punctuated as though it was a sentence. It is, of course, a noun phrase and the object of the verb *exspecto*. The chanter of the creed, according to my translation, hopes to see not only the resurrection of the dead but the life of the world to come.

The chief detail from the racing imagery produced in my mind by the last words of the creed was a certain movement performed by the rider of the winning horse. (I remind the reader that even when I chanted the creed as a child, my aim was far larger and more complex than merely to share in the success of the winner. If anyone knew the odds against the so-called dream-ending, I, the son of a reckless gambler on horses, knew them and suffered often as a result of their relentless operation. Even in my dreams I was realistic; the actual outcome was only seldom the desired.) Whether or not the winner was the hoped-for horse, its rider performed often a movement that was for me eloquent and yet provoking. A racing commentator might have described the movement simply thus: 'And So-and-so (rider of the winner) puts away the whip on So-and-so (winning horse).' In fact, I never heard any racing commentator use such words to describe the movement that I had in mind. The finish in my mind was usually what was called a hectic finish or a blanket finish or a desperate finish, and the commentator was so much occupied with merely naming the many horses vying for first place and, at the decisive moment, the seeming winner in his estimation that he could never have found the time to report such a detail as a movement performed by a jockey, even the jockey on the winning horse. In any case, the movement was not at all striking or worthy of reporting to persons listening to radio broadcasts. Only I, chanting the Nicene Creed in Latin and trying to call to mind a finish contested by numerous deserving contenders (and one especially hoped for) – only I was free to dwell on that movement; to see it re-enacted over and over, if I so chose, in the silence after the creed had ended and the field of horses had passed the winning-post. The putting-away of the whip always took place, in racing parlance, a stride before the post. Until the moment when he put the whip away, the rider had been using it repeatedly and with much force and had seemed to me, the spectator, to be aware of little else apart from the rhythmical straining of his body and that of the horse beneath him. Never having questioned any jockey about such matters, I supposed that the rider in my mind was only partly aware of his position in the field; that he knew he was gaining on the leaders but that he was no more sure than I of the final outcome. And yet, in the sort of race that had most meaning for me, all the straining and flailing of the rider of the eventual winner came to a graceful end in the shadows of the post, as a racing commentator might have described the place. The last arc of the rider's arm was shorter by far than the previous ten or twenty. Instead of flattening itself against the rump of the horse, the whip leaped nimbly back to its usual resting-place near the horse's shoulder while the hand holding it went back to the reins.

Et vitam venturi saeculi. Amen. In the most satisfying of all races, the rider put his whip to rest a moment before his horse reached the post a narrow winner in a blanket finish. Even before I had dropped my voice, the rider of the eventual winner had known that he had done enough: that the momentum of his horse would carry it through. Afterwards I was both teased and gratified for as long as I considered certain questions that I was never able to answer. How could the rider have known that the moment had arrived when he might safely put away the whip? How could he have seen from among the press of the onrushing horses, and while he crouched with his face against the mane of his horse and plied the whip with all the strength of his upper body, that although he had still not reached the finish-line, the race had been decided? What sign had the rider glimpsed from the side of his eye? What signal had he felt through the straining of the horse beneath him? What sound, even, might he have heard from the watching crowd?

During the twenty years when I was writing most of my published fiction, English was my only language. Nor did I ever feel that my native language was less than adequate for my purposes. Nor will I ever so feel. And yet, for much of my life I have felt that I lacked something by not being fluent in a second language. In 1951, when the first so-called New Australians arrived at my primary school, I persuaded a Maltese boy to teach me to speak his native language. Before he grew tired of it, he had taught me a good deal. I studied Latin and French successfully throughout secondary school. When I began at university in my late twenties, I was obliged to enrol in at least one unit of a foreign language. I chose Arabic and eventually completed a major in it. I was sorry to find that the examinations were only in writing. I never learned to converse in Arabic, although I was able to read and write it rather well. I recall little of the language today, however. Finally, when I was preparing to leave full-time employment in my mid-fifties, I bought two dictionaries and a teach-yourself book with an accompanying cassette and prepared to learn the Hungarian language.

I had seen photographs of Hungarian peasants in a *National Geographic* magazine when I was barely able to read. The photographs were illustrations for an article about Romania, and many years were to pass before I understood the details of the tragic separation of the millions of Hungarians in Transylvania from their compatriots after the First World War. I stared at pictures of peoples from many parts of the world in the second-hand *National Geographic* magazines that my father brought home from somewhere in the 1940s, but for reasons that I have never been able to explain, I was drawn to the Hungarians.

I cannot claim that I was a steadfast admirer during my childhood of Hungarian culture, but I remember instances when I thought of Hungary as having a claim on me. When I first saw pictures of the Great Plain of Hungary; when I first learned that the Hungarians had come from somewhere in Asia; when I learned of the affinity of Hungarians and the horse; and, above all, when I learned that the Hungarian language is more or less alone in the world, bearing little resemblance to any other language – at such times I heard in my mind something like the far-away or Sunday-afternoon sounds of my childhood; I heard myself speaking solemnly in Hungarian or even singing Hungarian songs, even though I knew not one word of the Magyar language.

I have never been one of those who speak condescendingly of the emotional turmoil of their adolescence. I am still some-times amazed at how I went on leading a normal-seeming life and passing examinations when my prevailing mood was for long periods one of utter confusion. The year 1956 was by far the most turbulent of my youth, and yet I turned away during the last months of that year from my private crises and pored over newspaper reports and photographic images of the Hungarian Revolution. No doubt, many other Australians shared my sympathy for the Hungarians at that time, but it seemed relevant to my own concerns that numbers of persons of my own age had lost their lives in the fighting. And whether I saw a photograph of her or whether I imagined her, a certain dark-haired young woman has appeared often in my mind ever since that time. I often asked myself what this sad-faced girl-ghost might have required of me. It would have been a hopeless task for me to try to learn even her name, let alone any of her history. There was only one thing that I might try to do for her, and that was to learn her language.

In 1977, I read for the first time a book titled *People of the Puszta*. It was an English translation of *Puszták Népe*, by Gyula Illyés, which was first published in Hungary in 1936. The book had such an effect on me that I later wrote a book of my own in order to relieve my feelings. Any reader interested in this matter is referred to *Inland*, 1988.

I have read several times during my life that this or that person was so impressed by this or that translation of this or that work of literature that the person afterwards learned the original language in order to read the original text. I have always been suspicious of this sort of claim, but the reader of this piece of writing need not doubt the truth of the following sentence. I was so impressed by the English version of *Puszták Népe* that I afterwards learned the language of the original and, as of now, have read a goodly part of it.

Even though I learned Hungarian for the first three years on my own, I was trying to learn it as a spoken language and not just a language of texts. I listened to my cassette and I learned by heart and recited often aloud all the passages of Hungarian dialogue in my textbook. I even listened to

Hungarian radio programmes, although the speakers were too fast for my comprehension. For three years I kept the Hungarian language confined within the four walls of my study, but then the language could bear its solitude no longer and broke free of me. On a memorable day in May, 1998, I found myself approaching the only Hungarian person I knew. He was a retired truck-driver from my own suburb. I had never so much as nodded to him previously, but on the memorable day I addressed him in my halting Hungarian. He embraced me as though I was a long-lost compatriot.

Joseph Kulcsar had had a humble occupation, but he was an outstanding figure in the Australian Hungarian community. Here, I mention only his extensive knowledge of Hungarian literature and history and his talents as an actor and a reciter of verse, although he was famous and respected for much else. But the day when I approached Joe in the street was a fateful day in more ways than one. Earlier that day, Joe had been diagnosed as having cancer. He lived for two years more. He was too ill and too tired during those years to teach me as much of his language as he would have liked, but I learned from him how the best of Hungarians love their country and its culture. I hope I may have learned from him also how to die bravely.

This is not meant to be a piece of scholarly writing; nor is it meant to be about the Hungarian language itself. I understand that scholars have for long debated the precise origins of the language – and of the Hungarian people themselves. It can be safely said that the language is a very old language. The main body of the Hungarian people brought the language through the Carpathians and into Central Europe in the ninth century of the modern era, but language and people had travelled before then an immense distance during many centuries from their place of origin somewhere in Asia. I like sometimes to look at my atlas and to read aloud the name of the city of Alma Ata in Kazakhstan. What I hear are two Hungarian words meaning 'Father of Apples'. Likewise the 'Bator' in the name of the capital city of Mongolia is the Hungarian word for 'brave'. Many Hungarian words and expressions set me wondering about the mysterious centuries before the people and their language arrived in Europe. I mention here only a Hungarian name for the Milky Way: *hadak útja*, the soldiers' road.

News of the Australian writer who taught himself Hungarian has by now reached members of the Hungarian community in Melbourne. I am touched by the joy of my new Hungarian friends that someone should brave the reputed difficulties of their language, which is so rarely studied outside their homeland. (In my experience, Hungarian is no more difficult than any other language known to me.) My friends at first suppose that I learned Hungarian so that I could enjoy the riches of Hungarian literature, and especially its poetry. Yes, one of my motives was to read *People of the Puszta* in the original, and yes, I have dipped into some most impressive works of literature. I have learned a number of Hungarian poems by heart, plus as many folk songs. And I have translated two poems for publication in HEAT, as some readers will be aware. But I try to explain to my friends what I am trying to explain to readers of this writing: that I learned Hungarian for purely personal reasons. My years-long enterprise might even be called an act of self-indulgence.

I learned to hear English and to speak English before I learned to read and to write English, but I long ago lost my awareness of English as a system of sounds. I learned to hear and to speak and to read and to write Hungarian all during the same time, but I am able with only a little effort, while I speak or recite or sing or merely listen, to become aware of Hungarian as mostly sounds. I can never be unaware of the written language. Somewhere in my mind the words go on appearing as writing. But the consistent sounds of Hungarian vowels and consonants and the strangely uniform pattern of stresses (only the first syllable of any word is stressed) take my attention away from the writing.

It may be an unhelpful comparison, but if an English word or phrase is a pane of clear glass with something called a meaning on its far side, a Hungarian word is a pane of coloured glass. The meaning on the other side of that glass is apparent to me, but I can never be unaware of the rich tints of the glass.

In the fourth year of my learning Hungarian and the first year of my friendship with Joe Kulcsar, I happened to hear from a community radio station a recitation of a long poem. Its title in English is 'Ode to the Hungarian Language'. The poet is György Faludy. The recitation lasted for perhaps eight minutes. It was sufficiently slow and clear for me to understand the outline of the poem, although much of the vocabulary was strange to me. What I most noticed was the sound of the poem. Some passages seemed to have been written especially to allow the sounds of Hungarian to come into play. Twenty years earlier, while I read an English translation of the prose of Gyula Illyés, I had vowed one day to read the original in Hungarian. Now, listening to György Faludy's 'Ode', I vowed to find the text and to learn it by heart.

On my next visit to Joe Kulcsar, I described what I had heard from the radio. I spoke as though Joe himself might not have heard of the poem. When I had finished speaking, Joe drew himself up in his chair and recited by heart the whole of 'Ode to the Hungarian Language'. Afterwards, he handed me a copy of the text so that I could learn it for myself, and before I left him that day he took me through the poem, explaining difficult passages and historical allusions.

One such allusion occurs in the very first lines of the poem and is relevant for my purposes in this writing. The first four lines may be paraphrased thus in English prose:

> Now, as the darkness of evening reaches into my room, you come to my mind, servant-girl of Saint Gerard, and your lips from which, under the trees at evening, the first sad Hungarian song burst out.

What these lines allude to, so Joe explained, is the earliest known reference to the distinctive music of the Hungarians. Saint Gerard was a Venetian missionary to Hungary during the eleventh century, when the nation was converting voluntarily to Christianity. A chronicle of those times reports Gerard's having heard one evening from his garden a Magyar servant-girl singing while she turned a hand-mill and his having been much affected, although he knew not a word of the Hungarian language.

I soon learned the poem by heart, although I could not say even today, several years later, that I have discovered all its meaning. During much of the poem, the poet considers by turns some of the lexical and grammatical components of his native language. Each of these he apprehends through his senses, so to speak. The ending of the past tense is the black crow's-wing of Hungarian history, for example, and the dark shadow of the gallows, the stake, and the cross. Adjectives are an endless flowering furrow. Obsolete words are deserted villages. But these few examples of mine can barely hint at the richness of the poem, which leads my thoughts through a quite different sequence of visual imagery whenever I recite it.

I have recited 'Ode to the Hungarian Language' many times since I first learned it. During most of my recitations I have had in mind one or another of the sequences of imagery mentioned in the previous paragraph, but I have not infrequently lost sight of the visual imagery and heard line after line as I first heard them from the radio; heard myself reciting only the sounds of the mysterious Magyar tongue. (In Hungarian, the same word, *nyelv*, means both 'language' and 'tongue'.) It has not yet happened to me, but it surely will happen to me that those sounds will bring to my mind images of a certain horse-race. Or, if the sounds of György Faludy's poem never give rise to those images, then the sounds of some other Hungarian poem, as yet unknown to me, surely will.

I have glimpsed already some of the details of that race. I know already that the name of the horse most prominent in the blanket finish of the race will be Angel's Son. The person looking out from the rear of the grandstand appears as a young female, perhaps the dark-haired young female denoted in so many Hungarian poems and songs by the phrase *barna kislány*. The rider of the horse Angel's Son will lower his whip gracefully an instant before the horse reaches the finish-line. What prompts the rider to do this is an event such as could happen only on a racecourse in the mind of such a person as can visualise only a racecourse whenever he looks for a meaning of meanings. The event may be either the rider's hearing in his own mind or, more likely, the person's hearing in his own mind as well as in the rider's mind one or another passage of Hungarian music in the traditional mode, which uses the same pentatonic scale as was used by the Catholic Church for all its Latin Hymns.

During one of my visits to Joe Kulcsar in the last year of his life, I tried to explain to him in Hungarian something of what I have tried to explain in this essay. He heard me out politely enough, but I wondered afterwards how much I had managed to explain. Then, a few months later, I read a report of an interview with Joe in the Hungarian-language weekly, *Magyar Élet*. The interviewer, Livia Bagin, at one point asked Joe about the Australian writer who was learning Hungarian from him. Joe spoke briefly about me and then, in one neat Hungarian sentence, reported what must have seemed to him the best summary of all he had heard from me about my reasons for making an old, Asian tongue my second language.

Azt mondja, hogy az angyalok mennyországban magyarul beszélnek.

He says that the angels in heaven speak Hungarian.

(*EGGPLANT DREAMING*, HEAT 5, NEW SERIES, 2003)

Dear readers,

As well as relying on bookshop sales, And Other Stories relies on subscriptions from people like you for many of our books, whose stories other publishers often consider too risky to take on.

Our subscribers don't just make the books physically happen. They also help us approach booksellers, because we can demonstrate that our books already have readers and fans. And they give us the security to publish in line with our values, which are collaborative, imaginative and 'shamelessly literary'.

All of our subscribers:

- receive a first-edition copy of each of the books they subscribe to
- are thanked by name at the end of our subscriber-supported books
- receive little extras from us by way of thank you, for example: postcards created by our authors

BECOME A SUBSCRIBER,
OR GIVE A SUBSCRIPTION TO A FRIEND

Visit andotherstories.org/subscriptions to help make our books happen. You can subscribe to books we're in the process of making. To purchase books we have already published, we urge you to support your local or favourite bookshop and order directly from them – the often unsung heroes of publishing.

OTHER WAYS TO GET INVOLVED

If you'd like to know about upcoming events and reading groups (our foreign-language reading groups help us choose books to publish, for example) you can:

- join our mailing list at: andotherstories.org
- follow us on Twitter: @andothertweets
- join us on Facebook: facebook.com/AndOtherStoriesBooks
- admire our books on Instagram: @andotherpics
- follow our blog: andotherstories.org/ampersand

This book was made possible thanks to the support of:

Aaron McEnery
Aaron Schneider
Abigail Walton
Ada Gokay
Adam Lenson
Adrian Astur
    Alvarez
Adriana Diaz Enciso
Ailsa Peate
Aisha McLean
Aisling Reina
Ajay Sharma
Alan Donnelly
Alan Hunter
Alan McMonagle
Alan Simpson
Alana Rupnarain
Alasdair Hutchison
Alastair Gillespie
Alessandra Lupski
    Raja
Alex Hoffman
Alex Ramsey
Alex Robertson
Alexander Barbour
Alexandra Citron
Alexandra Stewart
Alexandra Stewart
Alfred Birnbaum
Ali Conway
Ali Riley
Ali Smith
Alicia Bishop
Alison Winston
Aliya Rashid
Alyse Ceirante
Alyson Coombes
Alyssa Rinaldi
Alyssa Tauber
Amado Floresca
Amanda

Amanda Astley
Amanda Dalton
Amanda Greenstein
Amanda Read
Amanda Silvester
Amber Da
Amelia Ashton
Amelia Dowe
Amine Hamadache
Amitav Hajra
Amy Bojang
Amy Rushton
Amy Savage
Andra Dusu
Andrea Reece
Andre Marston
Andrew Jarred
Andrew Kerr-Jarrett
Andrew McCallum
Andrew Rego
Andriy Dovbenko
Andy Marshall
Angela Everitt
Anna Corbett
Anna Finneran
Anna Glendenning
Anna Gibson
Anna Milsom
Anna Pigott
Anna Zaranko
Anna-Maria Aurich
Anne Carus
Anne Craven
Anne Frost
Anne Higgins
Anne Sticksel
Anne Stokes
Anne-Marie
    Renshaw
Anneliese O'Malley
Anonymous

Anthea Morton
Anthony Brown
Anthony Cotton
Anthony Quinn
Anthony Thomas
Antoni Centofanti
Antonia Lloyd-Jones
Antonia Saske
Antony Pearce
Aoife Boyd
Archie Davies
Asako Serizawa
Asher Louise
    Sydenham
Ashleigh Sutton
Ashley Cairns
Asif Jehangir
Audrey Mash
Aviv Teller
Barbara Mellor
Barbara Robinson
Barbara Spicer
Barbara Wheatley
Barry John Fletcher
Bart Van Overmeire
Ben Schofield
Ben Thornton
Ben Walter
Benjamin Judge
Beryl Wesley and
    Kev Carmody
Bethlehem Attfield
Bettina Rogerson
Beverly Jackson
Bianca Winter
Bianca Duec
Bianca Jackson
Bill Fletcher
Birgitta Karlén
Bjørnar Djupevik
    Hagen

Bobbi Collins
Brendan Monroe
Briallen Hopper
Brian Anderson
Brian Byrne
Brian Callaghan
Brian Smith
Brigita Ptackova
Briony Norton
Bronx River Books
Brooke Williams
Bruna Rotzsch-
Thomas
Burkhard
Fehsenfeld
Caitlin Erskine
Smith
Caitlin Halpern
Caitriona Lally
Callie Steven
Callum Mackay
Cam Scott
Camilla Imperiali
Campbell McEwan
Carl Emery
Carol Mavor
Carol McKay
Carole Burns
Carolina Pineiro
Caroline Picard
Caroline Smith
Caroline West
Cassidy Hughes
Catherine
Blanchard
Catharine
Braithwaite
Catherine Lambert
Catherine Tolo
Catherine
Williamson
Catie Kosinski

Catriona Gibbs
Cecilia Rossi
Cecilia Uribe
Ceri Webb
Chantal Wright
Charlene Huggins
Charles Dee
Mitchell
Charles Fernyhough
Charles Raby
Charlie Cook
Charlie Errock
Charlotte Briggs
Charlotte Coulthard
Charlotte Holtam
Charlotte Middleton
Charlotte Ryland
Charlotte Whittle
China Miéville
Chris Gribble
Chris Gostick
Chris Lintott
Chris Maguire
Chris McCann
Chris & Kathleen
Repper-Day
Chris Stevenson
Chris Tomlinson
Christian Kopf
Christian
Schuhmann
Christina Moutsou
Christine Bartels
Christine Lewis
Christine and Nigel
Wycherley
Christof Bode
Christopher Allen
Christopher
Homfray
Christopher
Mitchell

Christopher Stout
Christopher Young
Ciara Ní Riain
Ciara Nugent
Claire Adams
Claire Brooksby
Claire Riley
Claire Tristram
Claire Williams
Clarice Borges
Cliona Quigley
Clive Bellingham
Clotilde Beaumont
Colin Denyer
Colin Hewlett
Colin Matthews
Collin Brooke
Connie Muttock
Courtney Lilly
Csilla Toldy
Cyrus Massoudi
Daisy Savage
Dale Wisely
Daniel Arnold
Daniel Coxon
Daniel Gillespie
Daniel Hahn
Daniel Ng
Daniel Oudshoorn
Daniel Pope
Daniel Raper
Daniel Stewart
Daniel Wood
Daniela Steierberg
Danny Millum
Danny Turze
Darina Brejtrova
Darren Davies
Darren Lerigo
Dave Lander
David Anderson
David Bevan

David Hebblethwaite
David Higgins
David Johnson-Davies
David F Long
David McIntyre
David Miller
David Musgrave
David Richardson
David Shriver
David Smith
David Steege
David Thornton
David Travis
David Willey
Davis MacMillan
Dawn Bass
Dean Taucher
Debbie Pinfold
Declan Gardner
Declan O'Driscoll
Deirdre Nic Mhathuna
Denis Larose
Denis Stillewagt & Anca Fronescu
Denton Djurasevich
Derek Taylor-Vrsalovich
Dermot McAleese
Diana Adell
Diana Cragg
Diana Digges
Diana Hutchison
Diana Romer
Diane Humphries
Dimitra Kolliakou:
Dinesh Prasad
Dominic Nolan
Dominick Santa Cattarina
Dominique Brocard
Duncan Clubb
Duncan Marks
Dyanne Prinsen
E Rodgers
Earl James
Ed Errington
Ed Tronick
Ed Burness
Ekaterina Beliakova
Eleanor Dawson
Eleanor Maier
Eleanor Rickards
Elie Howe
Elif Aganoglu
Elina Zicmane
Elisabeth Cook
Elisabeth Pike
Elizabeth Braswell
Elizabeth Cochrane
Elizabeth Dillon
Elizabeth Draper
Elizabeth Franz
Elizabeth Leach
Emilie Charnley & Simon Jones
Emily Webber
Emily Yaewon Lee & Gregory Limpens
Emily McCarthy
Emma Barraclough
Emma Bielecki
Emma Coulson
Emma Knock
Emma Louis Grove
Emma Page
Emma Perry
Emma Post
Emma Rhymer
Emma Selby
Emma Teale
Eric Anderson
Eric Tucker
Erin Cameron Allen
Esmée de Heer
Eve Anderson
Ewan Tant
F Gary Knapp
Felix Valdivieso
Finbarr Farragher
Finn Williamson
Fiona Galloway
Fiona Liddle
Fiona Quinn
Florence Reynolds
Florian Duijsens
Fran Sanderson
Frances Winfield
Francesca Brooks
Francis Mathias
Fred Nichols
Freddie Radford
Frederick Lockett
Friederike Knabe
Gabriel Martinez
Gabriel Vogt
Gabriela Lucia Garza de Linde
Gabrielle Crockatt
Garan Holcombe
Gareth Daniels
Gary Gorton
Gavin Smith
Gawain Espley
Genaro Palomo Jr
Genia Ogrenchuk
Geoff Thrower
Geoffrey Urland
Geoffrey Cohen
George Christie
George McCaig
George Stanbury
George Wilkinson
Georgia Dennison

German Cortez-Hernandez
Gerry Craddock
Gill Boag-Munroe
Gillian Grant
Gillian Spencer
Gillian Stern
Gordon Cameron
Gosia Pennar
Graham R Foster
Grant Rootes
Greg Bowman
Hadil Balzan
Hamish Russell
Hanna Randall
Hannah Dougherty
Hannah Ellul-Knight
Hannah Freeman
Hannah Mayblin
Hannah Procter
Hannah Vidmark
Hannah Jane Lownsbrough
Hans Lazda
Harriet Stiles
Harriet Wade
Haydon Spenceley
Hayley Newman
Heather Mason
Heather & Andrew Ordover
Heather Roche
Hebe George
Helen Berry
Helen Brady
Helen Brooker
Helen Collins
Helen Coombes
Helen Moor
Helen Peacock
Helen Wilson

Helen Wormald
Henrike Laehnemann
Henry Patino
Holly Down
HowardRobinson
Hugh Gilmore
Hugo Ferraz Gomes
Hyoung-Won Park
Ian Barnett
Ian C. Fraser
Ian Hagues
Ian Mond
Ian McMillan
Iciar Murphy
Ida Grochowska
Ifer Moore
Ilona Abb
Ingrid Olsen
Irene Croal
Irene Mansfield
Irina Tzanova
Isabel Adey
Isabella Livorni
Isabella Weibrecht
Isobel Foxford
J Collins
Jacinta Perez Gavilan Torres
Jack Brown
Jack Hargreaves
Jack Shinder
Jacob Blizard
Jacob Swan Hyam
Jacqueline Lademann
Jacqueline Ting Lin
Jacqueline Vint
Jacqui Jackson
Jake Nicholls
James Beck
James Crossley

James Cubbon
James Dahm
James Kinsley
James Lehmann
James Lesniak
James Mewis
James Portlock
James Russell
James Scudamore
James Ward
Jamie Veitch
Jamie Cox
Jamie Mollart
Jamie Walsh
Jane Anderton
Jane Bryce
Jane Dolman
Jane Fairweather
Jane Leuchter
Jane Roberts
Jane Roberts
Jane Woollard
Janne Støen
Jannik Lyhne
Jasmine Gideon
Jasmine Haniff
Jayne Watson
JC Sutcliffe
Jeff Collins
Jeff Questad
Jeff Van Campen
Jeffrey Danielson
Jeffrey Davies
Jenifer Logie
Jennifer Arnold
Jennifer Bernstein
Jennifer Fatzinger
Jennifer Harvey
Jennifer Higgins
Jennifer Robare
Jennifer Watts
Jennifer Wiegele

Jenny Huth
Jenny Newton
Jeremy Morton
Jeremy Koenig
Jerry Simcock
Jess Howard-
    Armitage
Jesse Coleman
Jessica Kibler
Jessica Laine
Jessica Martin
Jessica Queree
Jethro Soutar
Jill Westby
Jo Goodall
Jo Harding
Jo Woolf
Joanne Alder
Joanna Luloff
Joanne Osborn
Joanne Smith
Joao Pedro Bragatti
    Winckler
JoDee Brandon
Jodie Adams
Joe Bratccher
Joe Gill
Joel Swerdlow
Johanna Eliasson
Johannes Holmqvist
Johannes Menzel
John Bennett
John Berube
John Bogg
John Carnahan
John Conway
John Down
John Gent
John Hodgson
John Kelly
John Royley
John Shaw

John Steigerwald
John Winkelman
Jon Riches
Jon Talbot
Jonathan Blaney
Jonathan Fiedler
Jonathan Huston
Jonathan Watkiss
Jonathan Ruppin
Jonny Kiehlmann
Joseph Darlington
Joseph Schreiber
Joseph Hiller
Josh Calvo
Josh Sumner
Joshua Davis
Joshua McNamara
Joy Paul
Judith Gruet-Kaye
Judy Lee-Fenton
Judy Tomlinson
Julia Ellis Burnet
Julie Greenwalt
Julia Harkey
    D'Angelo
Julie Hutchinson
Julie Miller
Julia Peters
Julie Winter
Juliet and Nick
    Davies
Juliet Swann
Justin Ahlbach
Justine Goodchild
K Elkes
Kaarina Hollo
Karen Waloschek
Kasper Haakansson
Kasper Hartmann
Kat Burdon
Kate Attwooll
Kate Beswick

Kate Gardner
Kate Morgan
Kate Shires
Katharina Liehr
Katharine Freeman
Katherine Gray
Katherine
    Mackinnon
Katharine Robbins
Kathryn Dawson
Kathryn Edwards
Kathryn Oliver
Kathryn Williams
Katie Brown
Katie Grant
Katie Lewin
Katie Smart
Katie Wolstencroft
Katrina Thomas
Keith Walker
Kenneth Blythe
Kenneth Michaels
Kent McKernan
Kerry Parke
Kieran McGrath
Kieran Rollin
Kieron James
Kim McGowan
Kimberley Khan
Kirsten Hey
Kirsten Ward
Kirsty Doole
KL Ee
Klara Rešetič
Kris Ann Trimis
Kristin Djuve
Kristina Rudinskas
Krystine Phelps
Lana Selby
Lander Hawes
Lara Vergnaud
Laura Blasena

Laura Clarke
Laura Geraghty
Laura Lea
Laura Lonsdale
Laura Smith
Laura Williams
Lauren Carroll
Lauren Schluneger
Laurence Hull
Laurence Laluyaux
Laurie Sheck & Jim
  Peck
Leanne Radojkovich
Lee Harbour
Leeanne Parker
Leonie Smith
Lesli Green
Leslie Baillie
Leslie Benziger
Lewis Green
Lidia Winnicka
Liliana Lobato
Lillie Rosen
Lily Hersov
Lindsay Attree
Lindsay Brammer
Lindsey Ford
Linette Arthurton
  Bruno
Lisa Agostini
Lisa Fransson
Lisa Leahigh
Lisa Simpson
Lisa Weizenegger
Liz Clifford
Liz Ketch
Lola Boorman
Lori Frecker
Lorna Bleach
Lottie Smith
Louise Evans
Louise Greebverg

Louise Smith
Louise Whittaker
Luc Daley
Luc Verstraete
Lucas Elliott
Lucas J Medeiros
Lucia Rotheray
Lucile Lesage
Lucy Beevor
Lucy Moffatt
Luke Loftiss
Lydia Trethewey
Lydia Unsworth
Lynda Graham
Lynn Fung
Lynn Martin
M Manfre
Madeleine Maxwell
Madeline Teevan
Mads Pihl
  Rasmussen
Maeve Lambe
Maggie Humm
Maggie Redway
Mahan L Ellison & K
  Ashley Dickson
Malcolm and Rachel
  Alexander
Malgorzata Rokicka
Mandy Wight
Marcel Schlamowitz
Margaret Briggs
Margaret Jull Costa
Maria Ahnhem
  Farrar
Maria Lomunno
Maria Losada
Maria Pia Tissot
Marie Bagley
Marie Cloutier
Marie Donnelly
Marike Dokter

Marina Altoé
Marina Castledine
Marina Galanti
Marina Jones
Mario Cianci
Mario Sifuentez
Marjorie Schulman
Mark Dawson
Mark Harris
Mark Sargent
Mark Sheets
Mark Sztyber
Mark Waters
Marlene Adkins
Martha Nicholson
Martha Stevns
Martin Brown
Martin Jones
Martin Nathan
Mary Brockson
Mary Heiss
Mary O'Donnell
Mary Lynch
Mary Morton
Mary Ellen Nagle
Mary Nash
Mary Wang
Matt Jones
Matt Davies
Matt Greene
Matt O'Connor
Matthew Adamson
Matthew Armstrong
Matthew Banash
Matthew Black
Matthew Eatough
Matthew Francis
Matthew Gill
Matthew Lowe
Matthew Scott
Matthew Warshauer
Matthew Woodman

Matty Ross
Maurice Mengel
Max Cairnduff
Max Garrone
Max Longman
Max McCabe
Meaghan Delahunt
Meg Lovelock
Megan Oxholm
Megan Wittling
Melanie Tebb
Melissa Apfelbaum
Melissa Beck
Melissa Quignon-
　Finch
Meredith Jones
Meredith Martin
Meryl Wingfield
Michael Bichko
Michael Carver
Michael Dodd
Michael James
　Eastwood
Michael Gavin
Michael Holt
Michael Kuhn
Michael Moran
Michael
　Schneiderman
Michael Shayer
Michael Roess
Michelle
　Lotherington
Mike Turner
Milla Rautio
Milo Bettocchi
Miranda Gold
Miranda Persaud
Miriam McBride
Molly Foster
Moray Teale
Morgan Lyons

Moshe Prigan
Muireann Maguire
Myka Tucker-
　Abramson
Myles Nolan
N Tsolak
Nan Craig
Nancy Jacobson
Nancy Oakes
Natalie Charles
Natalie & Richard
Nathalie Atkinson
Nathan Weida
Neferti Tadiar
Neil George
Nicholas Brown
Nick Chapman
Nick Flegel
Nick James
Nick Nelson &
　Rachel Eley
Nick Sidwell
Nick Twemlow
Nicola Hart
Nicola Meyer
Nicola Mira
Nicola Sandiford
Nicole Matteini
Nigel Fishburn
Niki Davison
Nina Alexandersen
Nina Parish
Niven Kumar
Odilia Corneth
Olga Alexandru
Olga Zilberbourg
Olivia Payne
Olivia Turner
Pamela Ritchie
Pamela Tao
Patricia Appleyard
Patricia Aronsson

Patrick McGuinness
Paul Cray
Paul Daintry
Paul Scott
Paul Segal
Paul Jones
Paul Munday
Paul Myatt
Paula Edwards
Paula Enler
　Skyttberg
Pauline
　Westerbarkey
Pavlos Stavropoulos
Paz Berlese
Peggy Wood
Penelope Hewett
　Brown
Penny Simpson
Perlita Payne
Peter McBain
Peter McCambridge
Peter Rowland
Peter Vilbig
Peter Wells
Petra Stapp
Philip Carter
Philip Lewis
Philip Lom
Philip Warren
Philipp Jarke
Phoebe Harrison
Phoebe Lam
Phyllis Reeve
Pia Figge
Piet Van Bockstal
Pippa Tolfts
Polly Morris
PRAH Foundation
Rachael de Moravia
Rachael Williams
Rachel Carter

Rachel Goodall
Rachel Swearingen
Rachel Van Riel
Rachel Watkins
Ramon Bloomberg
Rea Cris
Rebecca Braun
Rebecca Carter
Rebecca Gaskell
Rebecca Moss
Rebecca Parry
Rebecca Rosenthal
Rhiannon
  Armstrong
Rhodri Jones
Rich Sutherland
Richard Ashcroft
Richard Bauer
Richard Carter
Richard Dew
Richard Gwyn
Richard Harrison
Richard Mansell
Richard Priest
Richard Shea
Richard Soundy
Rita O'Brien
Robert Gillett
Robert Hannah
Robert Hamilton
Robert Orton
Robert Wolff
Robin Taylor
Roger Newton
Roger Ramsden
Ronan Cormacain
Rory Williamson
Rosalind May
Rosalind Ramsay
Rosanna Foster
Rose Crichton
Rose Renshaw

Ross Trenzinger
Rowan Sullivan
Roxanne O'Del
  Ablett
Royston Tester
Roz Simpson
Ruby Kane
Rupert Ziziros
Ruth Morgan
Ruth Porter
Ryan Farrell
Sally Baker
Sally Warner
Sally Whitehill
Sam Gordon
Sam Reese
Sam Stern
Sam Scott Wood
Samantha Cox
Samuel Crosby
Santiago Sánchez
  Cordero
Sara Quiroz
Sara Sherwood
Sarah Arboleda
Scott Astrada
Sarah Barnes
Sarah Booker
Sarah Davies-
  Bennion
Sarah Edwards
Sarah Forster
Sarah Laycock
Sarah Lucas
Sarah Moss
Sarah Pybus
Sarah Roff
Sarah Ryan
Sarah Watkins
Sarah Wert
Scott Chiddister
Sez Kiss

Shannon Knapp
Sharon Dogar
Sharon Mccammon
Shaun Whiteside
Shauna Gilligan
Shauna Rogers
Sheridan Marshall
Sherman Alexie
Sheryl Jermyn
Shira Lob
Sian Hannah
Simon Clark
Simon Pitney
Simon Robertson
Simone Few
Simonette Foletti
SK Grout
Sonia McLintock
Sophia Wickham
Soren Murhart
ST Dabbagh
Stacy Rodgers
Stefanie Schrank
Stefano Mula
Stella Francis
Stephan Eggum
Stephanie Lacava
Stephen Cunliffe
Stephen
  Eisenhammer
Stephen Pearsall
Steven & Gitte
  Evans
Stu Sherman
Stuart Wilkinson
Sue Craven
Sunny Payson
Susan Howard
Susan Higson
Susie Roberson
Susie Sell
Susan Winter

Suzanne Kirkham
Suzanne Lee
Suzy Hounslow
Sylvie Zannier-Betts
Tamara Larsen
Tania Hershman
Tanya Royer
Tara Roman
Taylor Ffitch
Teresa Griffiths
Terry Kurgan
The Mighty Douche
    Softball Team
Therese Oulton
Thom Keep
Thomas Baker
Thomas Mitchell
Thomas Sharrad
Thomas van den
    Bout
Thomas Bell
Tiffany Lehr
Tim Kelly
Tim Scott
Tim Theroux
Tina Rotherham-

Winqvist
Toby Halsey
Toby Hyam
Toby Ryan
Tom Darby
Tom Doyle
Tom Franklin
Tom Gray
Tom Mooney
Tom Stafford
Tom Whatmore
Tony Bastow
Torna Russell-Hills
Tory Jeffay
Tracey Martin
Tracy Bauld
Tracy Heuring
Tracy Lee-Newman
Tracy Northup
Trevor Wald
Val Challen
Valerie Sirr
Valerie O'Riordan
Vanessa Dodd
Vanessa Heggie
Vanessa Nolan

Vanessa Rush
Vanessa
Veronica Barnsley
Vicki White
Vicky van der Luit
Victor Meadowcroft
Victoria Goodbody
Victoria Huggins
Victoria Maitland
Victoria Steeves
Vijay Pattisapu
Vikki O'Neill
Virginia Bond
Walter Smedley
Wendy Olson
Wendy Langridge
William
    Brockenborough
William Dennehy
William Franklin
William Schwaber
William Schwartz
Zachary Hope
Zara Rahman
Zoë Brasier
Zoe Thomas

CURRENT & UPCOMING BOOKS

GERALD MURNANE is the award-winning author of fifteen books in his native Australia. In 2019 *Tamarisk Row* and *Border Districts*, his first novel and his latest work of prose fiction respectively, were published to acclaim in the UK by And Other Stories, and are followed by *Collected Short Fiction* and *Invisible Yet Enduring Lilacs* in 2020. More titles will follow. Known for his passion for horse-racing and his refusal to travel outside Australia, Murnane lives in the remote village of Goroke in the northwest of Victoria, near the border with South Australia.